DEPARTMENT OF THE TREASURY
TECHNICAL EXPLANATION OF THE CONVENTION BETWEEN
THE UNITED STATES OF AMERICA
AND
THE SWISS CONFEDERATION
FOR THE AVOIDANCE OF DOUBLE TAXATION WITH
RESPECT TO TAXES ON INCOME
SIGNED AT WASHINGTON ON OCTOBER 2, 1996
AND
THE PROTOCOL
SIGNED AT WASHINGTON ON OCTOBER 2, 1996

DEPARTMENT OF THE TREASURY
TECHNICAL EXPLANATION OF THE CONVENTION BETWEEN
THE UNITED STATES OF AMERICA
AND
THE SWISS CONFEDERATION
FOR THE AVOIDANCE OF DOUBLE TAXATION WITH
RESPECT TO TAXES ON INCOME
SIGNED AT WASHINGTON ON OCTOBER 2, 1996
AND
THE PROTOCOL
SIGNED AT WASHINGTON ON OCTOBER 2, 1996

INTRODUCTION

This is a technical explanation of the Convention between the United States and Switzerland and the Protocol signed on October 2, 1996 ("the Convention" and "the Protocol"). References are made to the Convention between the United States and Switzerland with Respect to Taxes on Income and Certain other Taxes, signed on May 24, 1951 ("the prior Convention"). The Convention replaces the prior Convention.

Negotiations took into account the U.S. Treasury Department's current tax treaty policy, the Model Income Tax Convention on Income and on Capital, published by the OECD in 1992 and amended in 1994 and 1995 (the "OECD Model") and recent tax treaties concluded by both countries. References to the "U.S. Model" refer to the U.S. Treasury Department's Model Income Tax Convention of September 20, 1996, which was issued after negotiation of the Convention was completed, although prior drafts of the U.S. Model were available and taken into account in the course of negotiations.

In connection with the negotiation of the Convention and the Protocol, the negotiators developed and agreed upon a Memorandum of Understanding. The Memorandum of Understanding is a statement of intent setting forth a common understanding and interpretation of certain provisions of the Convention reached by the delegations of the Swiss Confederation and the United States acting on behalf of their respective governments. These understandings and interpretations are intended to give guidance both to the taxpayers and the tax authorities of both Contracting States in interpreting the relevant provisions of the Convention.

In the discussions of each Article in this explanation, the relevant portions of the Protocol and Memorandum of Understanding are discussed.

The Technical Explanation is an official guide to the Convention and Protocol. It reflects the policies behind particular Convention provisions, as well as understandings reached with respect to the application and interpretation of the Convention and Protocol. This technical explanation has been provided to Switzerland. References in the technical explanation to "he" or "his" should be read to mean "he or she" or "his or her."

Article 1 (Personal Scope)

Paragraph 1

Paragraph 1 of Article 1 provides that the Convention applies to residents of the United States or Switzerland except where the terms of the Convention provide otherwise. Under Article 4 (Resident) a person generally is treated as a resident of a Contracting State if that person is, under the laws of that State, liable to tax therein by reason of his domicile, residence or other similar criteria. If, however, a person is considered a resident of both Contracting States, a single State of residence (or no State of residence) is assigned under Article 4. This definition governs for all provisions of the Convention.

Certain provisions are applicable to persons who may not be residents of either Contracting State. For example, Article 19 (Government Service) may apply to an employee of a Contracting State who is resident in neither State. Paragraph 1 of Article 24 (Non-Discrimination) applies to nationals of the Contracting States, irrespective of their residence. Under Article 26 (Exchange of Information and Administrative Assistance), information may be exchanged with respect to residents of third states in certain cases.

Paragraph 2

Paragraph 2 contains the traditional saving clause found in U.S. tax treaties, and paragraphs 3(a) and (b) contain the exceptions to the saving clause. The United States reserves its right, except as provided in paragraph 3, to tax U.S. residents and citizens (including its former citizens) as provided in its internal law, notwithstanding any provisions of the Convention to the contrary. For example, if a resident of Switzerland performs independent personal services in the United States and the income from the services is not attributable to a fixed base in the United States, Article 14 (Independent Personal Services) would by its terms prevent the United States from taxing the income. If, however, the Swiss resident is also a citizen of the United States, the saving clause permits the United States to include the remuneration in the worldwide income of the citizen and subject it to tax under the normal Internal Revenue Code ("Code") rules (i.e., without regard to Code section 894(a)). For special foreign tax credit rules applicable to the U.S.

taxation of certain U.S. income of its citizens resident in Switzerland, see paragraph 3 of Article 23 (Relief from Double Taxation).

In many U.S. treaties the saving clause is reciprocal. Swiss tax policy does not call for such treatment, so the provision was made unilateral, affecting only U.S. taxing rights.

For purposes of the saving clause, "residence" is determined under Article 4 (Resident). Thus, if an individual who is not a U.S. citizen is a resident of the United States under the Code, and is also a resident of Switzerland under Swiss law, and that individual has a permanent home available to him in Switzerland and not in the United States, he would be treated as a resident of Switzerland under Article 4 and for purposes of the saving clause. The United States would not be permitted to apply its statutory rules to that person if they are inconsistent with the Convention. Thus, an individual who is a U.S. resident under the Code but who is deemed to be a resident of Switzerland under the tie-breaker rules of Article 4 would be subject to U.S. tax only to the extent permitted by the Convention. However, the person would be treated as a U.S. resident for U.S. tax purposes other than determining the individual's U.S. tax liability. For example, in determining under Code section 957 whether a foreign corporation is a controlled foreign corporation, shares in that corporation held by the individual would be considered to be held by a U.S. resident. As a result, other U.S. citizens or residents might be deemed to be United States shareholders of a controlled foreign corporation subject to current inclusion of Subpart F income recognized by the corporation. See, Treas. Reg. section 301.7701(b)-7(a)(3).

Under paragraph 2, the United States reserves its right to tax former U.S. citizens. Such a former citizen is taxable in accordance with the provisions of section 877 of the Code if his loss of citizenship had as one of its principal purposes the avoidance of tax. The United States generally treats an individual as having a principal purpose to avoid tax if (a) the average annual net income tax of such individual for the period of 5 taxable years ending before the date of the loss of status is greater than $100,000, or (b) the net worth of such individual as of such date is $500,000 or more. Although paragraph 2 does not specify a time frame in which this provision may be applied, under the Code rule, the United States retains its right to tax these former citizens for 10 years following the loss of citizenship.

Paragraph 3

Some provisions are intended to provide benefits to citizens and residents even if they do not exist under internal law. Paragraph 3 sets forth certain exceptions to the saving clause that preserve these benefits for citizens and residents of the United States. Subparagraph 3(a) lists certain provisions of the Convention that are applicable to all U.S. citizens and residents, despite the general saving clause rule of paragraph 2: (1) Paragraph 2 of Article 9 (Associated Enterprises) provides for correlative adjustments with respect to income tax due on profits reallocated under Article 9. (2) Paragraph 6 of Article 13 (Gains) permits the competent authorities to coordinate the timing of recognition of gain with respect to cross-border reorganizations. (3) Paragraph 7 of Article 13 (Gains) allows a resident to elect to be treated in his State of residence as having alienated and repurchased a property where the gain has been subject to tax in the other State. (4) Article 23 (Relief from Double Taxation) confirms the benefit of a foreign tax credit to U.S. citizens and residents for income taxes paid to Switzerland. (5) Article 24 (Non-Discrimination) requires one Contracting State to grant national treatment to residents and citizens of the other Contracting State in certain circumstances. Excepting this Article from the saving clause requires, for example, that the United States give such benefits to a resident or citizen of Switzerland even if that person is a citizen of the United States. (6) Article 25 (Mutual Agreement Procedure) may confer benefits on citizens and residents of a Contracting State. For example, the competent authorities are permitted to use a definition of a term which differs from the internal law definition, or they may refer an issue to an arbitration panel. As with the foreign tax credit, these benefits are intended to be granted by a State to its citizens and residents.

Subparagraph 3(b) provides a different set of exceptions to the saving clause. The benefits referred to are all intended to be granted to temporary residents of the United States (for example, holders of U.S. non-immigrant visas), but not to citizens or to persons who have acquired permanent residence in the United States. If beneficiaries of these provisions travel to the United States, and remain in the United States long enough to become residents under U.S. internal law, but do not acquire permanent residence status (i.e., they do not become "green card" holders) and are not citizens of the United States, the United States will continue to grant these benefits even if they conflict with the Code rules. The benefits preserved by this paragraph are the host country exemptions for the following items: Government service salaries and pensions under paragraphs 1 and 2 of Article 19 (Government Service and Social Security); certain income of students and trainees under Article 20 (Students and Trainees); and the income of diplomatic and consular officers under Article 27 (Members of Diplomatic Missions and Consular Posts); and the deductibility of pension fund contributions under paragraph 4 of Article 28 (Miscellaneous).

Article 2 (Taxes Covered)

This Article specifies the U.S. and Swiss taxes to which the Convention applies.

Paragraph 1

Like the OECD Model, but unlike the U.S. Model, Paragraph 1 contains a general description of the types of taxes that are covered (i.e., income taxes imposed on behalf of a Contracting State). Unlike the OECD Model, the Convention does not refer to taxes on capital, since there are no such taxes at the Federal level in the United States, and, therefore, no double taxation of capital can result.

The taxes specified in Article 2 are the covered taxes for all purposes of the Convention except for purposes of Article 24 (Non-discrimination), which applies with respect to taxes of all kinds imposed at any governmental level.

Paragraph 2

Subparagraph 2(a) specifies the existing Swiss taxes that are covered by the Convention. The taxes are all Swiss federal, cantonal and communal taxes on income, whether on total income, earned income, income from property or business profits. The Convention applies to Swiss federal taxes under the Federal Income Tax Act of 1990 and to cantonal and communal taxes under the cantonal income tax acts. However, as noted above, the Convention does not cover Swiss capital taxes.

Subparagraph 2(b) provides that the United States covered taxes are the Federal income taxes imposed by the Code, together with the excise taxes imposed on insurance premiums paid to foreign insurers (Code section 4371), and with respect to private foundations (Code sections 4940 through 4948). Although they may be regarded as income taxes, social security taxes (Code sections 1401, 3101 and 3111 and 3301) are specifically excluded from coverage under paragraph 1 of the Protocol. Income taxes on social security benefits are covered, however, and are dealt with in paragraph 4 of Article 19 (Government Service and Social Security). U.S. and Swiss social security taxes are dealt with in the bilateral Social Security Totalization Agreement of July 18, 1979, which entered into force on November 1, 1980 (as supplemented by the agreement of June 1, 1988 that entered into force on October 1, 1989).

The Convention applies to the federal excise tax on insurance premiums only to the extent that the risks covered by such premiums are not reinsured, directly or indirectly, with a person not entitled (under this or any other convention to which the United States is a party) to exemption from the tax. Providing Convention coverage for the U.S. insurance excise tax effectively exempts from the tax Swiss companies that insure U.S. risks, subject to the anti-conduit rule for reinsurance described above. This result is confirmed in paragraph 3 of the Protocol. Under the Code, the tax applies only to premiums that are not effectively connected to an active trade or business in the United States or that are exempt by treaty from net basis U.S. income tax (because they are not attributable to a permanent establishment). Under Article 7 (Business Profits), the United States does not subject the business profits of a Swiss enterprise to a tax that is covered by the Convention if the income of the enterprise is not attributable to a permanent establishment that the enterprise has in the United States. In contrast with this Convention, the prior Convention did not cover the insurance excise tax, allowing it to be imposed on premiums paid to Swiss insurers if such premiums were not attributable to a permanent establishment of the insurer in the United States.

In the Convention, unlike some U.S. treaties, the Accumulated Earnings Tax and the Personal Holding Company Tax are covered taxes because they are income taxes and they are not otherwise excluded from coverage. Under the Code, these taxes will not apply to most foreign corporations because of a statutory exclusion or the corporation's failure to meet a statutory requirement. In the few cases where the taxes may apply to a foreign corporation, the tax due is likely to be insignificant. Treaty coverage therefore confers little if any benefit on such corporations.

Paragraph 3

Under paragraph 3, the Convention will apply to any taxes that are identical, or substantially similar, to those enumerated in paragraph 2, and that are imposed in addition to, or in place of, the existing taxes after the date of signature of the Convention. The paragraph also provides that the U.S. and Swiss competent authorities will notify each other of significant changes in their taxation laws. The use of the term "significant" means that changes must be reported that are of significance to the operation of the Convention.

Article 3 (General Definitions)

Paragraph 1

Paragraph 1 of Article 3 defines a number of basic terms used in the Convention. Certain other terms are defined in other articles of the Convention. For example, the term "resident of a Contracting State" is defined in Article 4 (Resident). The term "permanent establishment" is defined in Article 5 (Permanent Establishment). The terms "dividends," "interest" and "royalties" are defined in Articles 10 (Dividends), 11 (Interest) and 12 (Royalties), respectively. The introduction to paragraph 1 makes clear that these definitions apply for all purposes of the Convention, unless the context requires otherwise. This latter condition allows flexibility in the interpretation of the treaty in order to avoid unintended results. Terms that are not defined in the Convention are dealt with in paragraph 2.

Subparagraph 1(a) defines the term "person" to include an individual, a partnership, a company, an estate, a trust and any other body of persons. The definition is significant for a variety of reasons. For example, under Article 4, only a "person" can be a "resident" and therefore eligible for most benefits under the Convention. Also, all "persons" are eligible to claim relief under Article 25 (Mutual Agreement Procedure).

This definition corresponds to the definition in the U.S. Model, which is more specific but not substantively different from the corresponding provision in the OECD Model. Unlike the OECD Model, it specifically includes a trust, an estate and a partnership. Since, however, the OECD Model's definition also uses the phrase "and any other body of persons," partnerships would be included, consistent with paragraph 2 of the Article, to the extent that they are treated as "bodies of persons" under the law of the Contracting State making the determination. Furthermore, because the OECD Model uses the term "includes," trusts and estates would be persons to the extent they are treated as such under that State's law. Under paragraph 2, the meaning of the terms "partnership," "trust" and "estate" would be determined by reference to the law of the Contracting State whose tax is being applied.

The term "company" is defined in subparagraph 1(b) as a body corporate or an entity treated as a body corporate for tax purposes under the laws of the Contracting State in which it is organized.

The terms "enterprise of a Contracting State" and "enterprise of the other Contracting State" are defined in paragraph 1(c) as an enterprise carried on by a resident of a Contracting State and an enterprise carried on by a resident of the other Contracting State, respectively. The term "enterprise" is not defined in the Convention, nor is it defined in the OECD Model or its Commentaries. Despite the absence of a clear, generally accepted meaning for the term "enterprise," the term is understood to refer to any activity or set of activities that constitute a trade or business.

An enterprise of a Contracting State need not be carried on in that State. It may be carried on in the other Contracting State or in a third state (e.g., a U.S. corporation doing all of its business in Switzerland would still be a U.S. enterprise).

The term "nationals," as it relates to both the United States and Switzerland, is defined in subparagraphs 1(d)(i) and (ii). This term is relevant for purposes of Articles 19 (Government Service) and 24 (Non-discrimination). A national of the United States is (1) a U.S. citizen as specified in subparagraph 1(d)(i), and (2) any legal person, partnership or association deriving its status as such from the law in force in the United States. A national of Switzerland is correspondingly defined as (1) an individual possessing the nationality of Switzerland, and (2) any legal person, partnership or association deriving its status as such from the law in force in Switzerland. This definition is closely analogous to that found in the OECD and U.S. Models.

The inclusion of juridical persons in the definition may have significance in relation to paragraph 1 of Article 24 (Non-Discrimination), which provides that nationals of one of the Contracting States may not be subject in the other State to any taxes or connected requirements that are other or more burdensome than those applicable to nationals of that other State who are in the same circumstances.

Paragraph 1(e) defines the term "international traffic." The term generally means any transport by a ship or aircraft, but does not include transport by a carrier that is an enterprise of one Contracting State when the vessel is operated solely between places within the other Contracting State. This definition is significant principally in the context of Article 8 (Shipping and Air Transport), and also is relevant to Article 13 (Gains) and Article 15 (Dependent Personal Services).

The exclusion from international traffic of transport solely between places within one of the Contracting States means, for example, that carriage of goods or passengers solely between New York and Chicago would not be treated as international traffic, even if carried by a Swiss carrier. The substantive taxing rules of the Convention relating to the taxation of income from transport, principally Article 8 (Shipping and Air Transport), therefore, would not apply to income from such carriage. Thus, if the carrier engaged in internal U.S. traffic were a resident of Switzerland (assuming that were possible under U.S. law), the United States would not be required to exempt the income from that transport under Article 8. The income would, however, be treated as business profits under Article 7 (Business Profits), and therefore would be taxable in the United States only if attributable to a U.S. permanent establishment of the foreign carrier, and then only on a net basis. The gross basis U.S. tax imposed by section 887 would never apply under the circumstances described.

If, however, goods or passengers are carried by a carrier resident in Switzerland from a non-U.S. port to, for example, New York, and some of the goods or passengers continue on to Chicago, the entire transport would be international traffic. This would be true if the international carrier transferred the goods at the U.S. port of entry from a ship to a land vehicle, or even if the overland portion of the trip in the United States was handled by an independent carrier under contract with the original international carrier, so long as both parts of the trip were reflected in original bills of lading. For this reason, the Convention, like the U.S. Model, refers, in the definition of "international traffic," to "such transport" being solely between places in the other Contracting State, while the OECD Model refers to the ship or aircraft being operated solely between such places. The Convention definition is intended to make clear that, as in the above example, even if the goods are carried on a different aircraft for the internal portion of the international voyage than is used for the overseas portion of the trip, the definition applies to that internal portion as well as the external portion.

Finally, a "cruise to nowhere," i.e., a cruise beginning and ending in a port in the same Contracting State with no stops in a foreign port, would not constitute international traffic.

Paragraphs 1(f)(i) and (ii) define the term "competent authority" of Switzerland and the United States, respectively. The competent authority of Switzerland is the Director of the Federal Tax Administration or his duly authorized representative. The U.S. competent authority is the Secretary of the Treasury or his delegate. The Secretary of the Treasury has delegated the competent authority function to the Commissioner of Internal Revenue, who has, in turn, redelegated the authority to the Assistant Commissioner (International). With respect to inter-pretative issues, the Assistant Commissioner acts with the concurrence of the Associate Chief Counsel (International) of the Internal Revenue Service.

The terms "Switzerland" and "United States" are defined in subparagraphs 1(g) and (h), respectively. The term "Switzerland" means the Swiss Confederation. The term "United States" is defined to mean the United States of America, not including Puerto Rico, the Virgin Islands, Guam or any other U.S. possession or territory. Under section 7701(a)(9) of the Code, the term "United States" includes the fifty states, the District of Columbia, and the territorial sea. When used geographically, the "United States" also includes the continental shelf. It is understood that the continental shelf is covered only to the extent that any U.S. taxation therein is in accordance with international law and U.S. tax law. Currently, U.S. tax law applies on the continental shelf only with respect to the exploration for and exploitation of mineral resources under section 638 of the Code.

Paragraph 2

Paragraph 2 provides that in the application of the Convention, any term used but not defined in the Convention generally will have the meaning that it has under the law of the Contracting State whose tax is being applied, unless the context requires otherwise. If a term is defined under both the tax and non-tax laws of a Contracting State, the definition in the tax law will take precedence over the definition in the non-tax laws. Finally, there also may be cases where the tax laws of a State contain multiple definitions of the same term. In such a case, the definition used for purposes of the particular provision at issue, if any, should be used.

If the meaning of a term cannot be readily determined under the law of a Contracting State, or if there is a conflict in meaning under the laws of the two States that creates difficulties in the application of the Convention, the competent authorities, as indicated in paragraph 3 f) of Article 25 (Mutual Agreement Procedure), may establish a common meaning in order to prevent double taxation or to further any other purpose of the Convention. This common meaning need not conform to the meaning of the term under the laws of either Contracting State.

It is understood that the reference in paragraph 2 to the internal law of a Contracting State means the law in effect at the time the Convention is being applied, not the law as in effect at the time the Convention was signed. The use of an "ambulatory definition," however, may lead to results that are at variance with the intentions of the negotiators and of the Contracting States when the Convention was negotiated and ratified. The reference in both paragraphs 1 and 2 to the "context otherwise requir[ing]" a definition different from the treaty definition, in paragraph 1, or from the internal law definition of the Contracting State whose tax is being imposed, under paragraph 2, refers to a circumstance where the result intended by the negotiators or by the Contracting States is different from the result that would obtain under either the paragraph 1 definition or the statutory definition. Thus, flexibility in defining terms is necessary and permitted.

Article 4 (Resident)

This Article sets forth rules for determining whether a person is a resident of a Contracting State for purposes of the Convention. As a general matter only residents of the Contracting States may claim the benefits of the Convention. The treaty definition of resident is to be used only for purposes of the Convention. The fact that a person is determined to be a resident of a Contracting State under Article 4 does not necessarily entitle that person to the benefits of the Convention. In addition to being a resident, a person also must qualify for benefits under Article 22 (Limitation on Benefits). The prior Convention contains no comprehensive definition of a resident.

The determination of residence for treaty purposes looks first to a person's liability to tax as a resident under the respective tax laws of the Contracting States. As a general matter, a person who, under those laws, is a resident of one Contracting State and not of the other need look no further. That person is a resident for purposes of the Convention of the State in which he is resident under internal law. If, however, a person is resident in both Contracting States under their respective taxation laws, the Article proceeds, where possible, to use tie-breaker rules to assign a single State of residence to such a person for purposes of the Convention.

Paragraph 1

Paragraph 1 defines the term "resident of a Contracting State." In general, this definition incorporates the definitions of residence in U.S. and Swiss law. Subparagraph (a) provides that a resident is a person who, under the laws of a Contracting State, is subject to tax there by reason of his domicile, residence, nationality, place of management, place of incorporation or any other similar criterion. Thus, residents of the United States include aliens who are considered U.S. residents under Code section 7701(b) unless the alien is a "green card" holder described in the following paragraph. Certain exceptions to this general rule are described below in relation to subparagraph 1(b) through (d) and paragraph 2.

Although the term "citizenship" does not appear among the explicit criteria of residence in the Convention, subparagraph 1(d)(i) of Article 3 (General Definitions) specifies that "nationality," which is included as a criteria of residence, means "citizenship" in the case of the United States. Accordingly, a U.S. citizen would generally be treated as a resident of the United States under the introductory language in subparagraph 1(a). However, subparagraph (a) also provides that a U.S. citizen or alien lawfully admitted for permanent residence (i.e., a "green card" holder) who is not, under the introductory language of paragraph 1 of this Article, an individual resident of Switzerland will be treated as a resident of the United States for purposes of the Convention, and, thereby entitled to treaty benefits, only if he has a substantial presence (see section 7701(b)(3)), permanent home or habitual abode in the United States. If, however, such an individual is a resident both of the United States and Switzerland under the general rule of paragraph 1(a), whether he is to be treated as a resident of the United States or of Switzerland for purposes of the Convention is determined by the tie-breaker rules of paragraph 3 of the Article, regardless of how close his nexus to the United States may be. However, the fact that a U.S. citizen who does not have close ties to the United States may not be treated as a U.S. resident under the Convention does not alter the application of the saving clause of paragraph 2 of Article 1 (Personal Scope) to that citizen. For example, a U.S. citizen who pursuant to the "citizen/green card holder" rule is not considered to be a resident of the United States still is taxable on his worldwide income under the generally applicable rules of the Code.

A nonresident alien individual may make an election under section 6013(g) of the Code to be treated as a U.S. resident in order to file a joint U.S. income tax return with a U.S. citizen or resident spouse. Paragraph 2 of the Protocol provides that residents of Switzerland making a spousal election under section 6013 of the Code will continue to be treated as residents of

Switzerland under the Convention and will be subject to U.S. taxation as U.S. residents. Thus, these individuals will be treated under the Convention in essentially the same way as U.S. citizens who are residents of Switzerland.

Certain entities that are nominally subject to tax but that in practice rarely pay tax also would generally be treated as residents and therefore accorded treaty benefits. For example, RICs, REITs and REMICs are all residents of the United States for purposes of the treaty. Although the income earned by these entities normally is not subject to U.S. tax in the hands of the entity, they are taxable to the extent that they do not currently distribute their profits, and therefore may be regarded as "liable to tax." They also must satisfy a number of requirements under the Code in order to be entitled to special tax treatment.

Subparagraph 1(b) provides that the Government of a Contracting State, a political subdivision or local authority of a Contracting State, or any agency or instrumentality of any such Government, subdivision or authority is a resident of a Contracting State. Paragraph 1 of the Memorandum of Understanding provides a definition of the term "Government" that includes not only agencies and instrumentalities but also certain non-commercial corporations owned by, and certain pension funds established for the benefit of employees of, the government of a Contracting State, political subdivision or local authority.

Subparagraph 1(c) provides that certain tax-exempt entities such as pension funds and charitable organizations will be regarded as residents. An entity will be described in this subparagraph if it is generally exempt from tax by reason of the fact that (1) it is organized and operated to perform a charitable or similar purpose or (2) it is organized and maintained exclusively to provide pension or other employee benefits and is established or sponsored by a person who, under the provisions of Article 4, is a resident of that State. The inclusion of this rule is intended to clarify the generally accepted practice of treating an entity that would be liable for tax as a resident under the internal law of a Contracting State but for a specific exemption from tax (either complete or partial) as a resident of that State for purposes of paragraph 1. The reference to a general exemption is intended to reflect the fact that under U.S. law, certain organizations that generally are considered to be tax-exempt entities may be subject to certain excise taxes or to income tax on their unrelated business income. Thus, a U.S. pension trust, or an exempt section 501(c) organization (such as a U.S. charity) that is generally exempt from tax under U.S. law is considered a resident of the United States for all purposes of the Convention.

Subparagraph 1(d) addresses special problems presented by fiscally transparent entities such as partnerships and certain estates and trusts that are not subject to tax at the entity level. Such entities are not residents under paragraph 1 because they are not liable for tax. However, subparagraph (d) provides that a partnership, estate or trust will be considered to be a resident to the extent that the income derived by the partnership, estate or trust is subject to tax in that State in the same manner as the income of a resident of that State, either in its hands or in the hands of its partners or beneficiaries. Example V of paragraph 4 of the Memorandum of Understanding confirms that this paragraph also applies to U.S. limited liability companies ("LLCs") that are treated as partnerships for U.S. tax purposes. Because such LLCs are not subject to tax in the United States, they are not considered to be residents of the United States under subparagraph 1. Under subparagraph (d), income derived by an LLC would be treated as derived by U.S. residents to the extent that U.S. residents were treated for U.S. tax purposes as deriving such income.

For example, if a Swiss corporation distributes a dividend to an entity that is fiscally transparent for U.S. purposes, the dividend will be considered to be derived by a resident of the United States only to the extent that the taxation laws of the United States treat one or more U.S. residents (whose status as U.S. residents is determined, for this purpose, under U.S. tax laws) as deriving the dividend income for U.S. tax purposes. In the case of a partnership, the persons who are, under U.S. tax laws, treated as partners of the entity would normally be the persons whom the U.S. tax laws would treat as deriving the dividend income through the partnership. Thus, it also follows that persons whom the U.S. treats as partners but who are not U.S. residents for U.S. tax purposes may not claim a benefit for the dividend paid to the entity under the Convention. Although these partners are treated as deriving the income for U.S. tax purposes, they are not residents of the United States for purposes of the treaty. If, however, the country in which they are treated as residents for tax purposes (as determined under the laws of that country) has an income tax convention with Switzerland, they may be entitled to claim a benefit under that convention. In contrast, if an entity is organized under U.S. laws and is classified as a corporation for U.S. tax purposes, dividends paid by a Swiss corporation to the U.S. entity will be considered derived by a resident of the United States since the U.S. corporation is treated under U.S. taxation laws as a resident of the United States and as deriving the income.

These results would obtain even if the entity were viewed differently under the tax laws of Switzerland (e.g., as not fiscally transparent in the first example above where the entity is treated as a partnership for U.S. tax purposes or as fiscally transparent in the second example where the entity is viewed as not fiscally transparent for U.S. tax purposes). These results also follow regardless of whether the entity is organized in the United States or in a third country or whether the entity is disregarded as a separate entity under the laws of one jurisdiction but not the other, such as a single owner entity that is viewed as a branch for U.S. tax purposes and as a corporation for Swiss tax purposes.

The language of paragraph 1(d) differs somewhat from the comparable provision in the U.S. Model. Switzerland wanted to ensure that partnerships organized in Switzerland would be treated as Swiss residents to the extent that the income of such partnerships is subject to tax in Switzerland in the same manner as income of Swiss corporations. Switzerland calculates the income of partnerships organized in Switzerland on a worldwide basis in the same manner as it calculates the income of a Swiss corporation. The only difference is that the liability, as so calculated, is then imposed on the partners in the partnership. Because the income earned by the partnership is subject to tax treatment in Switzerland that is similar to the tax treatment of income earned by Swiss resident corporations, the partnership is treated as resident in Switzerland. By contrast, partnerships conducting a business in Switzerland that are organized outside of

Switzerland are taxable in Switzerland only on the income attributable to the Swiss business; accordingly, the taxation of such a partnership is analogous to the taxation of a corporation that is not a resident of Switzerland. A partnership that is not organized in Switzerland will not be treated as a resident of Switzerland except to the extent that it has Swiss partners in whose hands the income is taxable as the income of a resident.

An item of income, profit or gain may be subject to tax as income, profit or gain of a resident of that State within the meaning of this provision even if the resident is not actually taxed on that particular item of income, profit or gain. For example, if dividend income received by a Swiss resident is exempt from tax in Switzerland as a result of the participation exemption, such income would be regarded as income or gain of a resident of Switzerland for purposes of the Convention.

Where income is derived through an entity organized in a third state that has owners resident in one of the Contracting States, the characterization of the entity in that third state is irrelevant for purposes of determining whether the resident is entitled to treaty benefits with respect to income derived by the entity.

This rule also applies to trusts (including family foundations treated as trusts) to the extent that they are fiscally transparent in their state of organization. For example, if X, a resident of Switzerland, creates a revocable trust and names persons resident in a third country as the beneficiaries of the trust, X would be treated as the beneficial owner of income derived from the United States under the Code's rules. If Switzerland had no rules comparable to those in sections 671 through 679 then it is possible that under the laws of Switzerland neither X nor the trust would be taxed on the income derived from the United States. In these cases subparagraph (d) provides that the trust's income would be regarded as being derived by a resident of Switzerland only to the extent that the laws of Switzerland treat its residents as deriving the income for tax purposes.

Paragraph 2

Paragraph 2 provides that a person who is liable to tax in a Contracting State only in respect of income from sources within that State will not be treated as a resident of that State for purposes of the Convention. Thus, a Swiss consular official who is posted in the United States, who may be subject to U.S. tax on U.S. source investment income, but is not taxable in the United States on his salary and non-U.S. source income under a consular convention, would not be considered a resident of the United States for purposes of the Convention. (See Code section 7701(b)(5)(B).) As another example, a Swiss enterprise with a permanent establishment in the United States is not, by virtue of that permanent establishment, a resident of the United States. The enterprise is subject to U.S. tax only with respect to its income attributable to the U.S. permanent establishment, not with respect to its worldwide income, as is a U.S. resident.

Paragraph 3

If, under the laws of the two Contracting States, and, thus, under paragraph 1, an individual is deemed to be a resident of both Contracting States, a series of tie-breaker rules are provided in paragraph 3 to determine a single State of residence for that individual. The first test is based on where the individual has a permanent home. If that test is inconclusive because the individual has a permanent home available to him in both States, he will be considered to be a resident of the Contracting State to which his personal and economic relations are closest (i.e., the location of his "center of vital interests"). If that test is also inconclusive, he will be treated as a resident of the Contracting State in which he maintains an habitual abode. If he has an habitual abode in both Contracting States or in neither of them, he will be treated as a resident of the State of which he is a national. If he is a national of both States or of neither, the matter will be considered by the competent authorities, who will assign a single State of residence.

Paragraph 4

Paragraph 4 seeks to settle dual-residence issues for persons other than individuals. A corporation is treated as resident in the United States if it is created or organized under the laws of the United States or a political subdivision. If the same test were used to determine corporate residence under Swiss law, dual corporate residence could not occur. However, under Swiss law, a corporation is treated as a resident of Switzerland if it is incorporated in Switzerland or if it has its place of effective management there. Dual residence, therefore, can arise if a corporation organized in the United States is managed in Switzerland. Paragraph 4 provides that, if a person other than an individual is resident in both the United States and Switzerland under paragraph 1, such person is treated as a resident of a Contracting State, and is, therefore, entitled to benefits of the Convention from the other State, only if and to the extent the competent authorities mutually agree. The competent authorities may limit the application of the Convention to the person to certain articles. If the competent authorities cannot reach agreement, the person will not be considered to be a resident of either the United States or Switzerland for any purposes of the Convention. They may, however, use the arbitration procedure of paragraph 6 of Article 25 (Mutual Agreement Procedure) to resolve the issue after the procedure is implemented in accordance with that Article.

Paragraph 5

Paragraph 5 provides that certain individuals are not treated as Swiss residents because they are not liable for tax on the same basis as other Swiss residents. This rule is necessary because Switzerland permits certain alien residents to elect not to be subject to the regularly applicable income tax on residents and instead to pay the "forfait tax." The base for the forfait tax is a multiple of rental value, deemed rental expenses or living expenses of the electing resident. It also includes all income that benefits from a reduction of tax under Swiss income tax conventions. A person who would otherwise be treated as a resident of Switzerland will not be considered a resident of Switzerland for purposes of the Convention if the person makes an election under Swiss law not to be subject to the income tax on residents.

Article 5 (Permanent Establishment)

This Article defines the term "permanent establishment," a term that is significant for several articles of the Convention. The existence of a permanent establishment in a Contracting State is necessary under Article 7 (Business Profits) for the taxation by that State of the business profits of a resident of the other Contracting State. Since the term "fixed base" in Article 14 (Independent Personal Services) is understood by reference to the definition of "permanent establishment," this Article is also relevant for purposes of Article 14. Articles 10, 11 and 12 (dealing with dividends, interest, and royalties, respectively) provide for reduced rates of tax at source on payments of these items of income to a resident of the other State only when the income is not attributable to a permanent establishment or fixed base that the recipient has in the source State. The concept is also relevant in determining which Contracting State may tax certain gains under Article 13 (Gains) and certain "other income" under Article 21 (Other Income).

This Article follows closely both the U.S. and OECD Model provisions. It does not differ significantly from the definition of a permanent establishment in the prior Convention.

Paragraph 1

The basic definition of the term "permanent establishment" is contained in paragraph 1. As used in the Convention, the term means a fixed place of business through which the business of an enterprise is wholly or partly carried on.

Paragraph 2

Paragraph 2 lists a number of types of fixed places of business that constitute a permanent establishment. This list is illustrative and non-exhaustive. According to paragraph 2, the term permanent establishment includes a place of management, a branch, an office, a factory, a workshop, and a mine, oil or gas well, quarry or other place of extraction of natural resources. As indicated in the OECD Commentaries (see paragraphs 4 through 8), a general principle to be observed in determining whether a permanent establishment exists is that the place of business must be "fixed" in the sense that a particular building or physical location is used by the enterprise for the conduct of its business, and that it must be foreseeable that the enterprise's use of this building or other physical location will be more than temporary.

Paragraph 3

Paragraph 3 provides rules to determine whether a building site, a construction or installation project, or a drilling rig or ship used for the exploration or development of natural resources constitutes a permanent establishment of the contractor, driller, etc. An activity is merely preparatory and does not create a permanent establishment under paragraph 4(e) unless the site, project, etc. lasts or continues for more than twelve months. It is only necessary to refer to "exploration or development" and not "exploitation" in this context because the definition of "permanent establishment" specifically includes exploitation activities under subparagraph (f) of paragraph 2. Thus, a drilling rig does not constitute a permanent establishment if a well is drilled in only six months, but if production begins in the following month the well becomes a permanent establishment at that time.

The twelve-month test applies separately to each site or project. The twelve-month period begins when work (including preparatory work carried on by the enterprise) physically begins in a Contracting State. A series of contracts or projects by a contractor that are interdependent both commercially and geographically are to be treated as a single project for purposes of applying the twelve-month threshold test. For example, the construction of a housing development would be considered a single project even if each house were constructed for a different purchaser. Several drilling rigs operated by a drilling contractor in the same sector of the continental shelf also normally would be treated as a single project.

If the twelve-month threshold is exceeded, the site or project constitutes a permanent establishment from the first day of activity. In applying this paragraph, time spent by a sub-contractor on a building site is counted as time spent by the general contractor at the site for purposes of determining whether the general contractor has a permanent establishment. However, for the sub-contractor itself to be treated as having a permanent establishment, the sub-contractor's activities at the site must last for more than 12 months. If a sub-contractor is on a site intermittently, time is measured from the first day the sub-contractor is on the site until the last day (i.e., intervening days that the sub-contractor is not on the site are counted) for purposes of applying the 12-month rule.

These interpretations of the Article are based on the Commentary to paragraph 3 of Article 5 of the OECD Model, which contains language almost identical to that in the Convention (except for the absence in the OECD Model of a rule for drilling rigs). These interpretations are consistent with the generally accepted international interpretation of the language in paragraph 3 of Article 5 of the Convention.

Paragraph 4

Paragraph 4 contains exceptions to the general rule of paragraph 1, listing a number of activities that may be carried on through a fixed place of business, but which nevertheless do not create a permanent establishment. The use of facilities solely to store, display or deliver merchandise belonging to an enterprise does not constitute a permanent establishment of that enterprise. The maintenance of a stock of goods belonging to an enterprise solely for the purpose of storage, display or delivery, or solely for the purpose of processing by another enterprise does not give rise to a permanent establishment of the first-mentioned enterprise. The maintenance of a fixed place of business solely for the purpose of purchasing goods or merchandise, or for collecting information, for the enterprise, or for other activities that have a preparatory or auxiliary character for the enterprise, such as advertising, or the supply of information or conduct of scientific research, will not constitute a permanent establishment of the enterprise. Thus, as explained in paragraph 22 of the OECD Commentaries, an employee of a news organization engaged merely in gathering information would not constitute a permanent establishment of the news organization.

Finally, subparagraph 4(f) provides that a combination of the activities described in the other subparagraphs of paragraph 4 will not give rise to a permanent establishment if the combination results in an overall activity that is of a preparatory or auxiliary character. This combination rule differs from that in the U.S. Model. In the U.S. Model, any combination of otherwise excepted activities is not deemed to give rise to a permanent establishment, without the additional requirement that the combination, as distinct from each constituent activity, be preparatory or auxiliary. It is assumed that if preparatory or auxiliary activities are combined, the combination generally will also be of a character that is preparatory or auxiliary. If, however, this is not the case, a permanent establishment may result from a combination of activities.

Paragraph 5

Paragraphs 5 and 6 specify when activities carried on by an agent on behalf of an enterprise creates a permanent establishment of that enterprise. Under paragraph 5, a dependent agent of an enterprise will be deemed to be a permanent establishment of the enterprise if the agent has and habitually exercises an authority to conclude contracts in the name of that enterprise. If, however, the agent's activities are limited to those activities specified in paragraph 4 which would not constitute a permanent establishment if carried on by the enterprise through a fixed place of business, the agent is not a permanent establishment of the enterprise.

Like the OECD Model, the Convention uses the term "in the name of that enterprise," rather than the term "binding on the enterprise," found in the U.S. Model. As indicated in paragraph 32 to the OECD Commentaries on Article 5, paragraph 5 of the Article is intended to encompass persons who have "sufficient authority to bind the enterprise's participation in the business activity in the State concerned." Therefore, the change to the U.S. Model is merely a clarification and does not result in a substantive difference between the two provisions.

The contracts referred to in paragraph 5 are those relating to the essential business operations of the enterprise, rather than ancillary activities. For example, if the agent has no authority to conclude contracts in the name of the enterprise with its customers for, say, the sale of the goods produced by the enterprise, but it can enter into service contracts in the name of the enterprise for the enterprise's business equipment used in the agent's office, this contracting authority would not fall within the scope of the paragraph, even if exercised regularly.

Paragraph 6

Under paragraph 6, an enterprise is not deemed to have a permanent establishment in a Contracting State merely because it carries on business in that State through an independent agent, including a broker or general commission agent, if the agent is acting in the ordinary course of its business. Thus, there are two conditions that must be satisfied: the agent must be both legally and economically independent of the enterprise, and the agent must be acting in the ordinary course of its business in carrying out activities on behalf of the enterprise.

Whether the agent and the enterprise are independent is a factual determination. Among the questions to be considered are the extent to which the agent operates on the basis of instructions from the enterprise. An agent that is subject to detailed instructions regarding the conduct of its operations or comprehensive control by the enterprise is not legally independent.

In determining whether the agent is economically independent, a relevant factor is the extent to which the agent bears business risk. Business risk refers primarily to risk of loss. An independent agent typically bears risk of loss from its own activities. In the absence of other factors that would establish dependence, an agent that shares business risk with the enterprise, or has its own business risk, is economically independent because its business activities are not integrated with those of the principal. Conversely, an agent that bears little or no risk from that activities it performs is not economically independent and therefore is not described in paragraph 6.

Another relevant factor in determining whether an agent is economically independent is whether the agent has an exclusive or nearly exclusive relationship with the principal. Such a relationship may indicate that the principal has economic control over the agent. A number of principals acting in concert also may have economic control over an agent. The limited scope of the agent's activities and the agent's dependence on a single source of income may indicate that the agent lacks economic independence. It should be borne in mind, however, that exclusivity is not in itself a conclusive test: an agent may be economically independent notwithstanding an exclusive relationship with the principal if it has the capacity to diversify and acquire other clients without substantial modifications to its current business and without substantial harm to its business profits. Thus, exclusivity should be viewed merely as a pointer to further investigation of the relationship between the principal and the agent. Each case must be addressed on the basis of its own facts and circumstances.

Paragraph 7

Paragraph 7 clarifies that a company that is a resident of a Contracting State is not deemed to have a permanent establishment in the other Contracting State merely because it controls, or is controlled by, a company that is a resident of that other Contracting State, or that carries on business in that other Contracting State. The determination whether a permanent establishment exists is made solely on the basis of the factors described in paragraphs 1 through 6 of the Article. Whether a company is a permanent establishment of a related company, therefore, is based solely on those factors and not on the ownership or control relationship between the companies.

Article 6 (Income from Real Property)

Paragraph 1

The first paragraph of Article 6 states the general rule that income of a resident of a Contracting State derived from real property situated in the other Contracting State may be taxed in the Contracting State in which the property is situated. The paragraph specifies that income from real property includes income from agriculture and forestry. Paragraph 3 clarifies that the income referred to in paragraph 1 also means income from any use of real property, including, but not limited to, income from direct use by the owner (in which case income may be imputed to the owner for tax purposes) and rental income from the letting of real property.

This Article does not grant an exclusive taxing right to the situs State; the situs States is merely given the primary right to tax. The Article does not impose any limitation in terms of rate or form of tax on the situs State, except that, as provided in paragraph 5, the situs State must allow the taxpayer an election to be taxed on a net basis.

Paragraph 2

The term "real property" is defined in paragraph 2 by reference to the internal law definition in the situs State. In the case of the United States, the term has the meaning given to it by Reg. § 1.897-1(b). In addition, the paragraph specifies certain classes of property which, regardless of internal law definitions, are to be included within the meaning of the term for purposes of the Convention. The definition of "real property" for purposes of Article 6, however, is more limited than the expansive definition of "real property situated in the Other Contracting State" in paragraph 2 of Article 13 (Gains), which includes not only real property itself, but certain interests in real property.

Paragraph 3

Paragraph 3 makes clear that all forms of income derived from the exploitation of real property are taxable in the Contracting State in which the property is situated. In the case of a net lease of real property, if a net election has not been made, the gross rental payment (before deductible expenses incurred by the lessee) is treated as the income from the property. Income from the disposition of an interest in real property, however, is not considered "derived" from real property and is not dealt with in this article. The taxation of that income is addressed in Article 13 (Gains). Also, the interest paid on a mortgage on real property and distributions by a U.S. Real Estate Investment Trust are not dealt with in Article 6.

Paragraph 4

This paragraph specifies that the basic rule of paragraph 1 (as elaborated in paragraph 3) applies to income from real property of an enterprise and to income from real property used for the performance of independent personal services. This clarifies that the situs country may tax the real property income of a resident of the other Contracting State in the absence of attribution to a permanent establishment or fixed base in the situs State. This provision represents an exception to the general rule under Articles 7 (Business Profits) and 14 (Independent Personal Services) that income must be attributable to a permanent establishment or fixed base, respectively, in order to be taxable in the situs state.

Paragraph 5

Paragraph 5 provides that a resident of one Contracting State that derives real property income from the other may elect to be subject to tax in the situs State on a net basis, as though the income were attributable to a permanent establishment or fixed base in that State. The election is subject to any procedures provided in the domestic law of the situs State. The election is binding for future taxable years to the extent so provided in the domestic law of the situs State. Thus, with respect to real property situated in the United States, revocation will be granted in accordance with the provisions of Treas. Reg. section 1.897-10(d)(2).

Article 7 (Business Profits)

This Article provides rules for the taxation by one of the Contracting States of the business profits of an enterprise of the other Contracting State.

Paragraph 1

Paragraph 1 contains the general rule that business profits of an enterprise of one Contracting State may not be taxed by the other Contracting State unless the enterprise carries on business in that other Contracting State through a permanent establishment (as defined in Article 5 (Permanent Establishment)) situated there. Where this condition is met, the State in which the permanent establishment is situated may tax the enterprise, but only on a net basis and only on the income that is attributable to the permanent establishment. This paragraph is identical to paragraph 1 of Article 7 of the OECD Model.

The rule in paragraph 1 differs from its counterpart in the prior Convention, which contained a limited force of attraction rule. That rule permits the United States to tax all of the U.S. source income of a Swiss enterprise with a permanent establishment even if the income is not attributable to the permanent establishment.

Paragraph 2

Paragraph 2 provides rules for the attribution of business profits to a permanent establishment. The Contracting States will attribute to a permanent establishment the profits that it would have earned had it been an independent entity engaged in the same or similar activities under the same or similar circumstances. This language incorporates the arm's-length concept in the calculation of the income of a permanent establishment. The computation of business profits attributable to a permanent establishment under this paragraph is subject to the rules of paragraph 3 for the allowance of expenses incurred for the purposes of earning the income.

The "attributable to" concept of paragraph 2 is analogous but not entirely equivalent to the "effectively connected" concept of Code section 864(c). The profits attributable to a permanent establishment may be from sources within or without a Contracting State. Thus, certain items of foreign source income described in Code section 864(c)(4)(B) may be attributed to a U.S. permanent establishment of a Swiss enterprise and subject to tax in the United States. This provision differs from the rule in the prior Convention, which does not include the "attributable to" concept and therefore does not allow the United States to tax non-U.S.-source income of a U.S. permanent establishment of a Swiss enterprise.

Paragraph 2 also provides that the business profits attributed to a permanent establishment include only those derived from that permanent establishment's assets or activities. This rule is consistent with the "asset use" and "business activities" test of section 864(c)(2). The OECD Model does not expressly provide such a limitation, although it generally is understood to be implicit in the paragraph 1 of Article 7 of the OECD Model. This provision was included to make it clear that the limited "force of attraction" rule of section 864(c)(3) is not incorporated into Article 7.

In determining the profits of a permanent establishment, only the portion of the income of the enterprise of which the permanent establishment is a part that is attributable to the actual activity of the permanent establishment is to be taken into account. Paragraph 2 of the Memorandum of Understanding reflects the understanding of the negotiators regarding the application of this principle to contracts for the survey, supply, installation or construction of industrial, commercial or scientific equipment or premises, or of public works. In that case, the profits attributable to the permanent establishment are determined on the basis of that part of the contract effectively carried out by the permanent establishment. The profits related to the part of the overall contract carried out by the head office are not subject to tax by the Contracting State in which the permanent establishment is situated. As noted above, profits may be attributable to the permanent establishment even if the profits are not from sources in the State in which the permanent establishment is located.

Paragraph 3 of Article 28 (Miscellaneous) refers to paragraphs 1 and 2 of Article 7 and incorporates into the Convention the rule of Code section 864(c)(6). Like the Code section on which it is based, it provides that any income, gain or expense attributable to a permanent establishment during its existence is taxable or deductible in the State in which the permanent establishment is situated even if the payment is deferred until after the permanent establishment no longer exists.

Paragraph 3

This paragraph is in substance the same as paragraph 3 of Article 7 of the OECD Model, although it is in some respects more detailed. Paragraph 3 of Article 7 provides that, in determining the business profits of a permanent establishment, deductions shall be allowed for expenses incurred for the purposes of the permanent establishment, thereby ensuring that business profits will be taxed on a net basis. This rule is not limited to expenses incurred exclusively for the purposes of the permanent establishment, but includes a reasonable allocation of expenses incurred for the purposes of the enterprise as a whole, or that part of the enterprise that includes the permanent establishment. Deductions are to be allowed regardless of which accounting unit of the enterprise books the expenses, so long as they are incurred for the purposes of the permanent establishment. Thus, a portion of the interest expense recorded on the books of the home office in one Contracting State may be deducted by a permanent establishment in the other if properly allocable thereto.

The paragraph specifies that the expenses that may be considered incurred for the purposes of the permanent establishment include expenses for research and development, interest and other similar expenses, as well as a reasonable amount of executive and general administrative expenses. This rule permits (but does not require) each Contracting State to apply the type of expense allocation rules provided by U.S. law (for example, in sections 1.861-8 and 1.882-5). It is expected that each State will use its own expense allocation rules for attributing expenses to a permanent establishment.

Paragraph 3 does not permit a deduction for expenses charged to a permanent establishment by another unit of the enterprise. Thus, a permanent establishment may not deduct a royalty deemed paid to the head office. Similarly, a permanent establishment may not increase its business profits by the amount of any notional fees for ancillary services performed for another unit of the enterprise, but also should not receive a deduction for the expense of providing such services, since those expenses were incurred for purposes of a business unit other than the permanent establishment.

Paragraph 4

Paragraph 4 corresponds to paragraph 4 of Article 7 of the OECD Model and provides that a Contracting State in certain circumstances may determine the profits attributable to a permanent establishment on the basis of an apportionment of the total profits of the enterprise. A total profits method may be employed by a Contracting State if it has been customary in that State to use the method even though the figure may differ to some extent from a separate enterprise method so long as the result is in accordance with the principles of Article 7 (i.e., the application of the arm's length standard). Although this paragraph is not included in the U.S. Model, this is not a substantive difference because the result provided by paragraph 4 is consistent with the rest of Article 7.

The U.S. view is that paragraphs 2 and 3 of Article 7 authorize the use of total profits methods independently of paragraph 4 of Article 7 of the OECD Model because total profits methods are acceptable methods for determining the arm's length profits of affiliated enterprises under Article 9. Accordingly, it is understood that, under paragraph 2 of the Convention, it is permissible to use methods other than separate accounting to estimate the arm's-length profits of a permanent establishment where it is necessary to do so for practical reasons, such as when the affairs of the permanent establishment are so closely bound up with those of the head office that it would be impossible to disentangle them on any strict basis of accounts. Any such approach, like any approach used under paragraph 4, is acceptable only if it approximates the result that would be achieved under an approach based on separate accounting. This view is confirmed by the OECD Commentaries on paragraphs 2 and 3 of Article 7.

Paragraph 5

Paragraph 5 provides that no business profits can be attributed to a permanent establishment merely because it purchases goods or merchandise for the enterprise of which it is a part. This rule is essentially identical to paragraph 5 of Article 7 of the OECD Model. This rule is applicable only to permanent establishment that perform functions for the enterprise in addition to purchasing. The income attribution issue does not arise if the sole activity of an office is the purchasing of goods or merchandise because, under subparagraph 4(d) of Article 5 (Permanent Establishment), there is no permanent establishment. A common fact pattern in which it does arise, however, is where a permanent establishment purchases raw materials for the enterprise's manufacturing operation conducted outside the United States and sells the manufactured output. While business profits may be attributable to the permanent establishment with respect to its sales activities, no profits are attributable to its purchasing activities.

Paragraph 6

Paragraph 6 tracks paragraph 6 of Article 7 of the OECD Model, providing that profits shall be determined by the same method of accounting each year, unless there is good reason to change the method used. This rule assures consistent tax treatment over time for permanent establishments. It limits the ability of both the Contracting State and the enterprise to change accounting methods to be applied to the permanent establishment. It does not, however, restrict a Contracting State from imposing additional requirements, such as the rules of Code section 481, to prevent amounts from being duplicated or omitted after a change in accounting method.

Paragraph 7

Paragraph 7 coordinates the provisions of Article 7 with other provisions of the Convention. Under this paragraph, when business profits include items of income that are dealt with separately under other articles of the Convention, the provisions of those articles will, except where they specifically provide to the contrary, take precedence over the provisions of Article 7. For example, the taxation of dividends will be determined by the rules of Article 10 (Dividends), and not by Article 7, unless, as provided in paragraph 5 of Article 10, the dividend is attributable to a permanent establishment, in which case the provisions of Article 7 apply. Thus, an enterprise of one State deriving dividends from the other State may not rely on Article 7 to exempt those dividends from tax at source if they are not attributable to a permanent establishment of the enterprise in the other State. By the same token, if the dividends are attributable to a permanent establishment in the other State, the dividends may be taxed on a net income basis at the source country's full corporate tax rate, rather than on a gross basis under Article 10.

As provided in Article 8 (Shipping and Air Transport), income derived from shipping and air transport activities described in that Article is taxable only in the country of residence of the enterprise regardless of whether it is attributable to a permanent establishment situated in the source State.

Paragraph 8

Consistent with the OECD Model, Article 7 does not include a general definition of the term "business profits." In the absence of such a definition, the term should be read to include all income derived from any trade or business. Paragraph 8, however, does specify that the term "business profits" as used in the Convention includes income from the rental of tangible movable property and income from the rental or licensing of cinematographic films or works on film, tape or other means of reproduction for use in radio or television broadcasting. The inclusion of these classes of income in business profits means that such income earned by a resident of a Contracting State can be taxed by the other Contracting State only if the income is attributable to a permanent establishment maintained by the resident in that other State, and, if the income is taxable, it can be taxed only on a net basis.

The term "business profits" is understood to include income attributable to notional principal contracts and other financial instruments to the extent that the income arises in connection with a trade or business of dealing in such instruments or is otherwise related to the trade or business carried on through the permanent establishment, as in the case of a notional principal contact entered into to hedge accounts receivable of the permanent establishment. Income derived from such instruments that is not related to such a trade or business is, unless specifically covered in another article, dealt with under Article 21 (Other Income).

Business profits also include income earned by an enterprise from the performance of personal services. Thus, a consulting firm resident in one Contracting State whose employees perform services in the other State through a permanent establishment may be taxed in that other State on a net basis under Article 7, and not under Article 14 (Independent Personal Services), which applies only to individuals. The salaries of the employees would be subject to the rules of Article 15 (Dependent Personal Services).

Relation to Other Articles

This Article is subject to the saving clause of paragraph 2 of Article 1 (Personal Scope) of the Convention. Thus, if a citizen of the United States who is a resident of Switzerland derives business profits from the United States that are not attributable to a permanent establishment in the United States, the United States may, subject to the special foreign tax credit rules of paragraph 3 of Article 23 (Relief from Double Taxation), tax those profits as part of the worldwide income of the citizen, notwithstanding the provision of paragraph 1 of this Article which would exempt such income from U.S. tax.

As with any benefit of the Convention, the benefits of this Article are also subject to the provisions of Article 22 (Limitation on Benefits). Thus, an enterprise that is a resident of Switzerland and that derives income effectively connected with a U.S. trade or business but that does not have a permanent establishment in the United States may not claim the benefits of Article 7 unless it qualifies for treaty benefits under Article 22.

Article 8 (Shipping and Air Transport)

This Article governs the taxation of profits from the operation of ships and aircraft in international traffic. The term "international traffic" is defined in subparagraph 1(e) of Article 3 (General Definitions).

Paragraph 1

Paragraph 1 provides that profits derived by an enterprise of a Contracting State from the operation in international traffic of ships or aircraft are taxable only in that Contracting State. Because paragraph 7 of Article 7 (Business Profits) defers to Article 8 with respect to shipping income, such income derived by a resident of one of the Contracting States may not be taxed in the other State even if the enterprise has a permanent establishment in that other State. Thus, if a U.S. airline has a ticket office in Switzerland, Switzerland may not tax the airline's profits attributable to that office under Article 7. Since entities engaged in international transportation activities normally will have many permanent establishments in a number of countries, the rule avoids difficulties that would be encountered in attributing income to multiple permanent establishments if the income were covered by Article 7 (Business Profits).

Paragraph 2

Paragraph 2 expands on the definition of income from the operation of ships or aircraft in international traffic beyond that implicit in the definition of "international traffic" in Article 3 (i.e., income from the operation of ships and aircraft in international traffic) to include other, related, classes of income that are exempt from tax under paragraph 1. In addition to income derived directly from the operation of ships and aircraft in international traffic, this definition also includes certain items of rental income that are closely related to those activities. First, income of an enterprise of a Contracting State from the rental of ships or aircraft on a full basis (i.e., with crew) when such ships or aircraft are used by the lessee in international traffic is income of the lessor from the operation of ships and aircraft in international traffic and, therefore, is exempt from tax in the other Contracting State under paragraph 1. Also, paragraph 2 encompasses income from the lease of ships or aircraft on a bareboat basis (i.e., without crew), when the income is incidental to other income of the lessor from the operation of ships or aircraft in international traffic.

Although not specifically stated in paragraph 2, consistent with the Commentary to Article 8 of the OECD Model, it is implicit that income earned by an enterprise from the inland transport of property or passengers within either Contracting State falls within Article 8 if the transport is undertaken as part of the international transport of property or passengers by the enterprise. Thus, if a U.S. airline contracts to carry property from Zurich to New York, and, as part of that contract, it transports the property by truck from Bern (the point of origin) to the Zurich airport (or it contracts with a trucking company to carry the property to the airport) the income earned by the U.S. airline from the overland leg of the journey would be taxable only in the United States.

In addition, certain non-transport activities that are an integral part of the services performed by a transport company are understood to be covered in paragraph 1, though they are not specified in paragraph 2. These include, for example, the performance of some maintenance or catering services by one airline for another airline, if these services are incidental to the provision of those services by the airline for itself. Income earned by concessionaires, however, is not covered by Article 8. These interpretations of paragraph 1 also are consistent with the Commentary to Article 8 of the OECD Model.

The scope of the income included within this Article by the terms of paragraph 2 is narrower than that in the U.S. Model, because it does not include income from the non-incidental leasing of ships and aircraft, or from the leasing of containers. Such income, under this Convention, is business profits, subject to tax under the provisions of Article 7 (Business Profits). As such, it is subject to source country tax only when it is attributable to a permanent establishment in that country, and, when taxable, is taxable on a net basis.

It is understood that if, for example, a bank is a resident of one of the States and has a permanent establishment in the other State, and that bank leases an aircraft to an airline in the other State, the rental income will not be attributable to the permanent establishment if the permanent establishment was not involved in negotiating or concluding the lease agreement. The rental income consequently will not be subject to tax by that other State.

Paragraph 3

This paragraph clarifies that the provisions of paragraph 1 also apply to profits derived by an enterprise of a Contracting State from participation in a pool, joint business or international operating agency. This refers to various arrangements for international cooperation by carriers in shipping and air transport. For example, airlines from two countries may agree to share the transport of passengers between the two countries. They each will fly the same number of flights per week and share the revenues from that route equally, regardless of the number of passengers that each airline actually transports. Paragraph 3 makes clear that with respect to each carrier the income dealt with in the Article is that carrier's share of the total transport, not the income derived from the passengers actually carried by the airline. This paragraph corresponds to paragraph 4 of Article 8 of the U.S. and OECD Models.

Relation to Other Articles

The taxation of gains from the alienation of ships or aircraft is not dealt with in this Article but in paragraph 4 of Article 13 (Gains).

As with other benefits of the Convention, the benefit of exclusive residence country taxation under Article 8 is available to an enterprise only if it is entitled to benefits under Article 22 (Limitation on Benefits).

This Article also is subject to the saving clause of paragraph 2 of Article 1 (Personal Scope) of the Convention. Thus, if a citizen of the United States who is a resident of Switzerland derives profits from the operation of ships or aircraft in international traffic, notwithstanding the exclusive residence country taxation in paragraph 1 of Article 8, the United States may, subject to the special foreign tax credit rules of paragraph 3 of Article 23 (Relief from Double Taxation), tax those profits as part of the worldwide income of the citizen. (This is an unlikely situation, however, because non-tax considerations (e.g., insurance) generally result in shipping activities being carried on in corporate form.)

Article 9 (Associated Enterprises)

This Article incorporates in the Convention the arm's-length principle reflected in the U.S. domestic transfer pricing provisions. It provides that when related enterprises engage in a trans-action on terms that are not arm's-length, the Contracting States may make appropriate adjust-ments to the taxable income and tax liability of such related enterprises to reflect what the income and tax of these enterprises with respect to the transaction would have been had there been an arm's-length relationship between them.

Paragraph 1

This paragraph is essentially the same as its counterpart in the OECD Model. It addresses the situation where an enterprise of a Contracting State is related to an enterprise of the other Contracting State, and there are arrangements or conditions imposed between the enterprises in their commercial or financial relations that are different from those that would have existed in the absence of the relationship. Under these circumstances, the Contracting States may adjust the income (or loss) of the enterprise to reflect what it would have been in the absence of such a relationship.

The paragraph identifies the relationships between enterprises that are necessary for application of the Article. As the Commentary to the OECD Model makes clear, the necessary element in these relationships is effective control, which is also the standard for purposes of section 482. Thus, the Article applies if an enterprise of one State participates directly or indirectly in the management, control, or capital of the enterprise of the other State. Also, the Article applies if any third person or persons participate directly or indirectly in the management, control, or capital of enterprises of different States. For this purpose, all types of control are included, i.e., whether or not legally enforceable and however exercised or exercisable.

The fact that a transaction is entered into between such related enterprises does not, in and of itself, mean that a Contracting State may adjust the income (or loss) of one or both of the enterprises under the provisions of this Article. If the conditions of the transaction are consistent with those that would be made between independent persons, the income arising from that transaction should not be subject to adjustment under this Article.

Similarly, the fact that associated enterprises may have concluded arrangements, such as cost sharing arrangements or general services agreements, is not in itself an indication that the two enterprises have entered into a non-arm's-length transaction that should give rise to an adjustment under paragraph 1. Both related and unrelated parties enter into such arrangements (e.g., joint venturers may share some development costs). As with any other kind of transaction, when related parties enter into an arrangement, the specific arrangement must be examined to see whether or not it meets the arm's-length standard. In the event that it does not, an appropriate adjustment may be made, which may include modifying the terms of the agreement or recharacterizing the transaction to reflect its substance.

It is understood that nothing in paragraph 1 limits the rights of the Contracting States to apply their internal law provisions relating to adjustments between related parties. Such adjustments -- the distribution, apportionment, or allocation of income, deductions, credits or allowances -- are permitted even if they are different from, or go beyond, those authorized by paragraph 1 of the Article, as long as they accord with the general principles of paragraph 1, i.e., that the adjustment reflects what would have transpired had the related parties been acting at arm's length. For example, while paragraph 1 explicitly allows adjustments of deductions in computing taxable income, it does not deal with adjustments to tax credits. It does not, however, preclude such adjustments if they can be made under internal law. The OECD Model reaches the same result. See paragraph 4 of the Commentaries to Article 9.

It is understood that the "commensurate with income" standard for determining appropriate transfer prices for intangibles, added to Code section 482 by the Tax Reform Act of 1986, was designed to operate consistently with the arm's-length standard. The implementation of this standard in the section 482 regulations is in accordance with the general principles of paragraph 1 of Article 9 of the Convention, as interpreted by the OECD Transfer Pricing Guidelines.

This Article also permits tax authorities to deal with thin capitalization issues. They may, in the context of Article 9, scrutinize more than the rate of interest charged on a loan between related persons. They also may examine the capital structure of an enterprise in determining whether a related party loan would have been made at arm's length, whether a payment in respect of that loan should be treated as interest, and, if it is treated as interest, under what circumstances interest deductions should be allowed to the payor. Paragraph 2 of the Commentaries to Article 9 of the OECD Model, together with the U.S. observation set forth in paragraph 15, sets forth a similar understanding of the scope of Article 9 in the context of thin capitalization.

Paragraph 2

Paragraph 2 provides that where a Contracting State proposes to make an adjustment to the profits of an enterprise of that State that is consistent with the provisions of paragraph 1 (i.e., that was appropriate to reflect arm's length conditions), and the associated enterprise in the other State has been subject to tax on those same profits, the competent authorities of the Contracting States may consult pursuant to Article 25 (Mutual Agreement Procedure) about whether to make an adjustment to the profits of the associated enterprises. If the competent authorities agree on the adjustments, then each Contracting State shall make the agreed adjustment to the extent provided by Article 25.

As explained in the OECD Commentaries, Article 9 leaves the treatment of "secondary adjustments" to the laws of the Contracting States. When an adjustment under Article 9 has been made, one of the parties will have in its possession funds that it would not have if the original relationship had been at arm's length. The question arises as to how to treat these funds. In the United States the general practice is to treat such funds as a dividend or contribution to capital, depending on the relationship between the parties. Under certain circumstances, the parties may be permitted to restore the funds to the party that would have the funds at arm's length, and to establish an account payable pending restoration of the funds. See, Rev. Proc. 65-17, 1965-1 C.B. 833.

The problem of compensating payments is dealt with differently under Swiss law. Switzerland permits a Swiss subsidiary to make a compensating payment to a U.S. parent corporation to reflect an adjustment of profits from the subsidiary to the parent without the imposition of a Swiss withholding tax if the compensating payment is made out of a reserve against the adjustment previously established by the subsidiary. Because such payment is not considered a dividend, Switzerland does not impose a withholding tax.

Relation to Other Articles

The saving clause of paragraph 2 of Article 1 (Personal Scope) does not apply to paragraph 2 of Article 9 because of the exceptions to the saving clause in paragraph 3(a) of Article 1. Thus, even if the statute of limitations has run, a refund of tax can be made in order to implement a correlative adjustment arising under paragraph 2 of Article 9. Statutory or procedural limitations, however, cannot be overridden to impose additional tax, because, under paragraph 1 of Article 28 (Miscellaneous) the Convention cannot restrict any statutory benefit.

Article 10 (Dividends)

Article 10 provides rules for the taxation of dividends arising in one Contracting State to a beneficial owner that is a resident of the other Contracting State. The Article provides for full residence country taxation of such dividends and a limited source-State right to tax. Article 10 also provides rules for the imposition of a tax on branch profits by the United States. Finally, the Article prohibits a State from imposing a tax on dividends paid by a company resident in the other Contracting State that are neither paid to a resident of the first-mentioned State nor attributable to a permanent establishment in that State and from imposing taxes, other than a branch profits tax in the case of the United States, on undistributed earnings of such companies.

Paragraph 1

The right of a shareholder's country of residence to tax dividends arising in the source country is preserved by paragraph 1, which permits a Contracting State to tax its residents on dividends which they beneficially own. The Convention does not limit the rate or the manner in which the tax may be imposed.

Paragraph 2

The State of source may also tax dividends beneficially owned by a resident of the other State, subject to the limitations in paragraph 2. Generally, the source State's tax is limited to 15 percent of the gross amount of the dividend paid. If, however, the beneficial owner of the dividends is a company resident in the other State that holds directly at least 10 percent of the voting stock of the company paying the dividend, then the source State's tax is limited to 5 percent of the gross amount of the dividend. Indirect ownership of voting shares (through tiers of corporations) and direct ownership of non-voting shares are not taken into account for purposes of determining eligibility for the 5 percent direct dividend rate. Shares are considered voting shares if they provide the power to elect, appoint or replace the person, or a majority of the board of persons, exercising the powers ordinarily exercised by the board of directors of a U.S. corporation.

The benefits of paragraph 2 may be granted at the time of payment by means of reduced withholding at source. It also is consistent with the paragraph for tax to be withheld at the time of payment at full statutory rates, and the treaty benefit to be granted by means of a subsequent refund.

Paragraph 2 does not affect the taxation of the profits out of which the dividends are paid. The taxation by a Contracting State of the income of its resident companies is governed by the internal law of the Contracting State, subject to the provisions of paragraph 4 of Article 24 (Non-discrimination).

The term "beneficial owner" is not defined in the Convention, and is, therefore, defined as under the internal law of the country imposing tax (i.e., the source country). The beneficial owner of the dividend for purposes of Article 10 is the person to which the dividend income is attributable for tax purposes under the laws of the source State. Thus, if a dividend paid by a corporation that is a resident of one of the States (as determined under Article 4 (Residence)) is received by a nominee or agent that is a resident of the other State on behalf of a person that is not a resident of that other State, the dividend is not entitled to the benefits of this Article. However, a dividend received by a nominee on behalf of a resident of that other State would be entitled to benefits. These limitations are confirmed by paragraph 12 of the OECD Commentaries to Article 10. See also, paragraph 24 of the OECD Commentaries to Article 1 (General Scope).

Companies holding shares through fiscally transparent entities such as partnerships are considered for purposes of this paragraph to hold their proportionate interest in the shares held by the intermediate entity. As a result, companies holding shares through such entities may be able to claim the benefits of subparagraph (a) under certain circumstances. The lower rate applies when the company's proportionate share of the shares held by the intermediate entity meets the 10 percent voting stock threshold. Whether this ownership threshold is satisfied may be difficult to determine and often will require an analysis of the partnership or trust agreement.

Paragraph 2 contains special rules that modify the general maximum rates of tax at source provided in paragraph 2 in particular cases. These special rules deny the lower direct investment withholding rate of paragraph 2(a) for dividends paid by a U.S. Regulated Investment Company (RIC) or a U.S. Real Estate Investment Trust (REIT). The rules also deny the benefits of both subparagraphs (a) and (b) of paragraph 2 to dividends paid by REITs in certain circumstances, allowing them to be taxed at the U.S. statutory rate (30 percent). The United States limits the source tax on dividends paid by a REIT to the 15 percent rate when the beneficial owner of the dividend is an individual resident of Switzerland that owns a less than 10 percent interest in the REIT. These exceptions to the general rules of paragraph 2 have been part of U.S. tax treaty policy since 1988.

The denial of the 5 percent withholding rate at source to all RIC and REIT shareholders, and the denial of the 15 percent rate to all but small individual shareholders of REITs is intended to prevent the use of these entities to gain unjustifiable source taxation benefits for certain shareholders. For example, a corporation resident in Switzerland that wishes to hold a diversified portfolio of U.S. corporate shares may hold the portfolio directly and pay a U.S. withholding tax of 15 percent on all of the dividends that it receives. Alternatively, it may acquire a diversified portfolio by purchasing shares in a RIC. Since the RIC may be a pure conduit, there may be no U.S. tax costs to interposing the RIC in the chain of ownership. Absent the special rule in paragraph 2, use of the RIC could transform portfolio dividends, taxable in the United States under the Convention at 15 percent, into direct investment dividends taxable at only 5 percent.

Similarly, a resident of Switzerland directly holding U.S. real property would pay U.S. tax either at a 30 percent rate on the gross income or at graduated rates on the net income (up to 39.6 percent in the case of individuals and up to 35 percent in the case of corporations). As in the preceding example, by placing the real property in a REIT, the investor could transform real estate income into dividend income, taxable at the rates provided in Article 10, significantly reducing the U.S. tax burden that otherwise would be imposed. To prevent this circumvention of U.S. rules applicable to real property, most REIT shareholders are subject to 30 percent tax at source. However, since a relatively small individual investor might be subject to a U.S. tax of 15 percent of the net income even if he earned the real estate income directly, individuals who hold less than a 10 percent interest in the REIT remain taxable at source at a 15 percent rate.

Paragraph 3

Paragraph 3 provides that, notwithstanding the source-country right to tax granted in paragraph 2, the source country may not tax dividends beneficially owned by certain residents of the other Contracting State that are described in paragraph 4(b) of Article 28 (Miscellaneous). This exemption applies only to beneficial owners of dividends that are pension plans or other retirement arrangements of the other Contracting State that have been determined by the competent authority of the source country to correspond to pension plans or other retirement arrangements of the source country. The beneficial owner of the dividend (i.e., the pension plan) is denied the exemption if it controls the company paying the dividend. Individual savings plans, such as individual retirement accounts in the United States and contributory private savings plans in Switzerland, are not pension plans or other retirement arrangements for purposes of this paragraph.

Paragraph 4

Paragraph 4 defines the term dividends broadly and flexibly. The definition is intended to cover all arrangements that yield a return on an equity investment in a corporation as determined under the tax law of the state of source, as well as arrangements that might be developed in the future.

The term dividends includes income from shares, or other corporate rights that are not treated as debt under the law of the source State, that participate in the profits of the company. Paragraph 4 of the Protocol states that participation in the profits of the obligor is a factor to be taken into account in determining whether an instrument nominally characterized as a debt-claim should be treated for purposes of the Convention as equity. The term also includes income that is subjected to the same tax treatment as income from shares by the law of the State of source. Thus, a constructive dividend that results from a non-arm's length transaction between a corporation and a related party is a dividend. In the case of the United States the term dividend includes amounts treated as a dividend under U.S. law upon the sale or redemption of shares or upon a transfer of shares in a reorganization. See, e.g., Rev. Rul. 92-85, 1992-2 C.B. 69 (sale of foreign subsidiary's stock to U.S. sister company is a deemed dividend to extent of subsidiary's and sister's earnings and profits). Further, a distribution from a U.S. publicly traded limited partnership, which is taxed as a corporation under U.S. law, is a dividend for purposes of Article 10. However, a distribution by a limited liability company is not taxable by the United States under Article 10, provided the limited liability company is not characterized as an association taxable as a corporation under U.S. law. Finally, a payment denominated as interest that is made by a thinly capitalized corporation may be treated as a dividend to the extent that the debt is recharacterized as equity under the laws of the source State.

Paragraph 5

Paragraph 5 excludes from the general source country limitations of paragraph 2 dividends paid with respect to holdings that form part of the business property of a permanent establishment or a fixed base. Such dividends will be taxed on a net basis using the rates and rules of taxation generally applicable to residents of the State in which the permanent establishment or fixed base is located, as modified by the Convention.

The rule in paragraph 3 of Article 28 (Miscellaneous) dealing with deferred income and expenses of a permanent establishment or fixed base applies to paragraph 5 of this Article. Thus, dividend income that is attributable to a permanent establishment or fixed base, but is deferred until after the permanent establishment or fixed base no longer exists, may nevertheless be taxed by the State in which the permanent establishment or fixed base was located.

Paragraph 6

A State's right to tax dividends paid by a company that is a resident of the other Contracting State is restricted by paragraph 6 to cases in which the dividends are paid to a resident of that State or are attributable to a permanent establishment or fixed base in that State. Thus, a State may not impose a "secondary" withholding tax on dividends paid by a nonresident company out of earnings and profits from that State. In the case of the United States, paragraph 6, therefore, overrides the taxes imposed by sections 871 and 882(a) on dividends paid by foreign corporations that have a U.S. source under section 861(a)(2)(B).

Paragraph 7

Paragraph 7 permits the United States to impose a branch profits tax on a corporation resident in Switzerland The tax is in addition to other taxes permitted by the Convention.

The United States may impose a branch profits tax on a Swiss corporation if the corporation has income attributable to a permanent establishment in the United States, derives income from real property in that State that is taxed on a net basis under Article 6 (Income from Real Property), or realizes gains taxable in that State under paragraph 1 or 3 of Article 13. The tax is limited, however, to the aforementioned items of income that are included in the "dividend equivalent amount."

Paragraph 7 permits the United States generally to impose its branch profits tax on a Swiss corporation to the extent of the corporation's (i) business profits that are attributable to a permanent establishment in the United States, (ii) income that is subject to taxation on a net basis because the corporation has elected under section 882(d) of the Code to treat income from real property not otherwise taxed on a net basis as effectively connected income and (iii) gain from the disposition of a United States Real Property Interest, other than an interest in a United States Real Property Holding Corporation. The United States may not impose its branch profits tax on the business profits of a Swiss corporation that are effectively connected with a U.S. trade or business but that are not attributable to a permanent establishment and are not otherwise subject to U.S. taxation under Article 6 or paragraph 1 of Article 13.

Paragraph 5 of the Protocol provides an explanation of the term "dividend equivalent amount" used in paragraph 7. The Protocol makes clear that the term has the same meaning in the Convention that it has under section 884 of the Code, as amended from time to time, provided the amendments are consistent with the purpose of the branch profits tax. Generally, the dividend equivalent amount for a particular year is the income described above that is included in the corporation's effectively connected earnings and profits for that year, after payment of the corporate tax under Articles 6, 7 or 13, reduced for any increase in the branch's U.S. net equity during the year and increased for any reduction in its U.S. net equity during the year. U.S. net equity is U.S. assets less U.S. liabilities. The dividend equivalent amount for any year approximates the dividend that a U.S. branch office would have paid during the year if the branch had been operated as a separate U.S. subsidiary company.

Paragraph 8

Paragraph 8 provides that the branch profits tax permitted by paragraph 7 shall not be imposed at a rate exceeding the direct investment dividend withholding rate of five percent, as specified in subparagraph 2(a) of Article 10 (Dividends).

Relation to Other Articles

Notwithstanding the foregoing limitations on source country taxation of dividends, the saving clause of paragraph 2 of Article 1 (Personal Scope) permits the United States to tax dividends received by its residents and citizens, subject to the special foreign tax credit rules of paragraph 3 of Article 23 (Relief from Double Taxation), as if the Convention had not come into effect.

The benefits of this Article are also subject to the provisions of Article 22 (Limitation on Benefits). Thus, if a Swiss resident is the beneficial owner of dividends of a U.S. corporation, in order to receive the benefits of this Article, the shareholder must qualify for treaty benefits under at least one of the tests of Article 22.

Article 11 (Interest)

Article 11 specifies the taxing jurisdictions over interest income of the States of source and residence and defines the terms necessary to apply the article.

Paragraph 1

This paragraph grants to the State of residence the exclusive right, subject to exceptions provided in paragraphs 3 and 6, to tax interest beneficially owned by its residents.

The term "beneficial owner" is not defined in the Convention, and is, therefore, defined as under the internal law of the country imposing tax (i.e., the source country). The beneficial owner of interest for purposes of Article 11 is the person to which the interest income is attributable for tax purposes under the laws of the source State. Thus, if interest arising in one of the States is received by a nominee or agent that is a resident of the other State on behalf of a person that is not a resident of that other State, the interest is not entitled to the benefits of this Article. However, interest received by a nominee on behalf of a resident of that other State would be entitled to benefits. These limitations are confirmed by paragraph 8 of the OECD Commentaries to Article 11. See also, paragraph 24 of the OECD Commentaries to Article 1 (General Scope).

Paragraph 2

The term "interest" as used in Article 11 is defined in paragraph 2 to include, inter alia, income from debt claims of every kind, whether or not secured by a mortgage. Penalty charges for late payment of taxes are excluded from the definition of interest. Interest that is paid or accrued subject to a contingency is within the ambit of Article 11. Although Paragraph 4 of the Protocol specifies that participation in the profits of an enterprise is a factor in determining whether an instrument nominally characterized as a debt-claim should be treated instead as equity, if the instrument is in fact treated as a debt instrument, then income from the instrument is covered under this Article. The term does not, however, include amounts that are treated as dividends under Article 10 (Dividends). In this regard, paragraph 4 of the Protocol states that participation in the profits of the obligor is a factor to be taken into account in determining whether an instrument nominally characterized as a debt-claim should be treated for purposes of the Convention as equity. The term interest includes excess inclusions with respect to residual interests in real estate mortgage investment conduits, in order that the special rules of Paragraph 6 will apply to such amounts.

The term interest also includes amounts treated as income from money lent under the law of the State in which the income arises. Thus, for purposes of the Convention amounts that the United States will treat as interest include (i) the difference between the issue price and the stated redemption price at maturity of a debt instrument, i.e., original issue discount (OID), which may be wholly or partially realized on the disposition of a debt instrument (section 1273), (ii) amounts that are imputed interest on a deferred sales contract (section 483), (iii) amounts treated as OID under the stripped bond rules (section 1286), (iv) amounts treated as original issue discount under the below-market interest rate rules (section 7872), (v) a partner's distributive share of a partnership's interest income (section 702), (vi) the interest portion of periodic payments made under a "finance lease" or similar contractual arrangement that in substance is a borrowing by the nominal lessee to finance the acquisition of property, and (vii) amounts included in the income of a holder of a residual interest in a REMIC (section 860E), because these amounts generally are treated as interest under U.S. tax law.

Paragraph 3

Paragraph 3 provides an exception to the exclusive residence taxation rule of paragraph 1 in cases where the beneficial owner of the interest carries on business through a permanent establishment in the State of source or performs independent personal services from a fixed base situated in that State and the interest is attributable to that permanent establishment or fixed base. In such cases the provisions of Article 7 (Business Profits) or Article 14 (Independent Personal Services) will apply and the State of source will retain the right to impose tax on such interest income.

In the case of a permanent establishment or fixed base that once existed in the State but that no longer exists, the provisions of paragraph 3 also apply, by virtue of paragraph 3 of Article 28 (Miscellaneous), to interest that would be attributable to such a permanent establishment or fixed base if it did exist in the year of payment or accrual. The Convention therefore preserves the right of the United States to tax interest paid or accrued with respect to a deferred transaction described in section 864(c)(6). See the Technical Explanation of paragraph 3 of Article 28.

Paragraph 4

Paragraph 4 provides that in cases involving special relationships between persons, Article 11 applies only to that portion of the total interest payments that would have been made absent such special relationships (i.e., an arm's-length interest payment). Any excess amount of interest paid remains taxable according to the laws of the United States and Switzerland, respectively, with due regard to the other provisions of the Convention. Thus, if the excess amount would be treated under the source country's law as a distribution of profits by a corporation, such amount could be taxed as a dividend rather than as interest, but the tax would be subject, if appropriate, to the rate limitations of paragraph 2 of Article 10 (Dividends).

The term "special relationship" is not defined in the Convention. In applying this paragraph the United States considers the term to include the relationships described in Article 9, which in turn corresponds to the definition of "control" for purposes of section 482 of the Code.

This paragraph does not address cases where, owing to a special relationship between the payer and the beneficial owner or between both of them and some other person, the amount of the interest is less than an arm's-length amount. In those cases a transaction may be characterized to reflect its substance and interest may be imputed consistent with the definition of interest in paragraph 2. The United States would apply section 7872 of the Code to determine the amount of imputed interest in those cases.

Paragraph 5

Paragraph 5 limits the right of one Contracting State to impose tax on interest payments made by a company that is a resident of the other Contracting State. Such a tax may be imposed only on interest paid by a permanent establishment of such company located in the first-mentioned State, or interest paid out of income, taxed on a net basis by the first-mentioned State, that is described in Article 6 (Income from Real Property) or paragraph 1 of Article 13 (Gains). Thus, for example, if a Swiss company derives income from the United States that is subject to the United States branch profits tax because either the company has a permanent establishment in the United States, or even if it has no permanent establishment in the United States, because such company makes an election to be taxed on a net basis under section 882(d) of the Code or it disposes of a United States Real Property Interest, the United States retains the right to tax interest payments made by such company under section 884(f)(1). Such interest paid to a resident of Switzerland, however, is not subject to U.S. tax by virtue of paragraph 1 of Article 11. If the interest is paid to a resident of a third State with which the United States has an income tax treaty, the provisions of that treaty may determine if and how the tax is to be imposed.

Paragraph 6

Paragraph 6 provides anti-abuse exceptions to the exemption provided by the United States under paragraph 1 with respect to two classes of U.S. source interest payments.

The first exception, in subparagraph (a) of paragraph 5, deals with so-called "contingent interest." Under this provision interest arising in the United States that does not qualify as portfolio interest under section 871(h) or 881(c) and that is determined by reference to the receipts, sales, income, profits or other cash flow of the debtor or a related person, to any change in the value of any property of the debtor or a related person or to any dividend, partnership distribution or similar payment made by the debtor to a related person, and paid to a resident of Switzerland also may be taxed in the United States according to its laws, (i.e., at a rate of 30 percent of the gross payment).

The second exception, in subparagraph (b) of paragraph 5, is consistent with the policy of Code sections 860E(e) and 860G(b) that excess inclusions with respect to a real estate mortgage investment conduit (REMIC) should bear full U.S. tax in all cases. Without a full tax at source foreign purchasers of residual interests would have a competitive advantage over U.S. purchasers at the time these interests are initially offered. Also, absent this rule the U.S. fisc would suffer a revenue loss with respect to mortgages held in a REMIC because of opportunities for tax avoidance created by differences in the timing of taxable and economic income produced by these interests.

Relation to Other Articles

Notwithstanding the foregoing limitations on source country taxation of interest, the saving clause of paragraph 2 of Article 1 (Personal Scope) permits the United States to tax its residents and citizens, subject to the special foreign tax credit rules of paragraph 3 of Article 23 (Relief from Double Taxation), as if the Convention had not come into force.

As with other benefits of the Convention, the benefits of exclusive residence State taxation of interest under paragraph 1 of Article 11 are available to a resident of the other State only if that resident is entitled to those benefits under the provisions of Article 22 (Limitation on Benefits).

Article 12 (Royalties)

Article 12 specifies the taxing jurisdiction over royalties of the States of residence and source and defines the terms necessary to apply the article.

Paragraph 1

Paragraph 1 grants to the State of residence of the beneficial owner of royalties the exclusive right to tax royalties arising in the other Contracting State, subject to exceptions provided in paragraph 3 (for royalties that are attributable to a permanent establishment or a fixed base).

The term "beneficial owner" is not defined in the Convention, and is, therefore, defined as under the internal law of the country imposing tax (i.e., the source country). The beneficial owner of royalties for purposes of Article 12 is the person to which the royalty income is attributable for tax purposes under the laws of the source State. Thus, if royalties arising in one of the States is received by a nominee or agent that is a resident of the other State on behalf of a person that is not a resident of that other State, the royalties are not entitled to the benefits of this Article. However, royalties received by a nominee on behalf of a resident of that other State would be entitled to benefits. These limitations are confirmed by paragraph 4 of the OECD Commentaries to Article 12. See also, paragraph 24 of the OECD Commentaries to Article 1 (General Scope).

Paragraph 2

The term "royalties" as used in the Convention is defined in paragraph 2 to include payments of any kind received as a consideration for the use of, or the right to use, any copyright of a literary, artistic, or scientific work; for the use of, or the right to use, any patent, trademark, design or model, plan, secret formula or process, or other like right or property; or for information concerning industrial, commercial, or scientific experience.

The term "royalties" also includes gain derived from the alienation of any right or property that would give rise to royalties, if the gain is contingent on the productivity, use, or further alienation thereof. If a gain is not contingent, it is dealt with under Article 13 (Gains).

The term royalties is defined in the Convention and therefore is generally independent of domestic law. Certain terms used in the definition are not defined in the Convention, but these may be defined under domestic tax law. For example, the term "secret process or formulas" is found in the Code, and its meaning has been elaborated in the context of sections 351 and 367. See Rev. Rul. 55-17, 1955-1 C.B. 388; Rev. Rul. 64-56, 1964-1 C.B. 133; Rev. Proc. 69-19, 1969-2 C.B. 301.

The term "industrial, commercial, or scientific experience" (sometimes referred to as "know-how") has the meaning ascribed to it in paragraph 11 of the Commentary to Article 12 of the OECD Model Convention. Consistent with that meaning, the term may include information that is ancillary to a right otherwise giving rise to royalties, such as a patent or secret process.

Know-how also may include, in limited cases, technical information that is conveyed through technical or consultancy services. It does not include general educational training of the user's employees, nor does it include information developed especially for the user, for example, a technical plan or design developed according to the user's specifications.

The term "royalties" does not include professional services (such as architectural, engineering, legal, managerial, medical and software development services) that merely apply the general body of knowledge of that profession. For example, income from the design of a refinery by an engineer or the production of a legal brief by a lawyer is not income from know-how taxable under Article 12, but services taxable under either Article 14 (Dependent Personal Services) or Article 15 (Independent Personal Services). Professional services may be embodied in property that gives rise to royalties, however. Thus, if a professional contracts to develop a patentable property and retains rights in the resulting property under the development contract, subsequent license payments made for those rights would be royalties.

Computer software generally is protected by copyright laws around the world. Under the Convention consideration received for the use or the right to use computer software is treated either as royalties or as business profits, depending on the facts and circumstances of the transaction giving rise to the payment. It is also understood that payments received in connection with the transfer of so-called "shrink-wrap" computer software are treated as business profits.

Consideration for the use or right to use motion pictures, or films, tape, or other means of reproduction in radio or television broadcasting, is specifically excluded from the definition of royalties. Such payments, therefore, are to be treated as business profits, taxable by the source country only when attributable to a permanent establishment in that country. The reference to "other means of reproduction" is to take account of subsequent technological advances in the field of radio and television broadcasting.

The exclusion for certain reproductions of performances does not extend beyond motion pictures. For example, if an artist who is resident in one Contracting State records a musical performance in the other Contracting State, retains a copyrighted interest in a recording, and receives payments for the right to use the recording based on the sale or public playing of the re-cording, then the right of such other Contracting State to tax those payments is governed by Article 12. See Boulez v. Commissioner, 83 T.C. 584 (1984), aff'd, 810 F.2d 209 (D.C. Cir. 1986).

The term "royalties" also does not include income from the leasing of tangible property.

Paragraph 3

This paragraph provides an exception to the rule of paragraph 1 that gives the state of residence exclusive taxing jurisdiction in cases where the beneficial owner of the royalties carries business through a permanent establishment in the state of source or performs independent personal services from a fixed base situated in that state and the royalties are attributable to that permanent establishment or fixed base. In such cases the provisions of Article 7 (Business Prof-its) or Article 14 (Independent Personal Services) will apply.

The provisions of paragraph 3 of Article 28 (Miscellaneous) dealing with deferred income and expenses of a permanent establishment or fixed base apply to paragraph 3 of this Article. Thus, royalty income that is attributable to a permanent establishment or fixed base and accrues while the permanent establishment or fixed base exists, but is received after the permanent estab-lishment or fixed base no longer exists, may nevertheless be taxed by the State in which the permanent establishment or fixed base was located under the provisions of Articles 7 (Business Profits) or 14 (Independent Personal Services), respectively, and not under this Article.

Paragraph 4

Paragraph 4 provides that in cases involving special relationships between the payor and beneficial owner of royalties, Article 12 applies only to the extent the royalties would have been made absent such special relationships (i.e., an arm's-length royalty). Any excess amount of royalties paid remains taxable according to the laws of the two Contracting States with due regard to the other provisions of the Convention. If, for example, the excess amount is treated as a distribution of corporate profits under domestic law, such excess amount will be taxed as a dividend rather than as royalties, but the tax imposed on the dividend payment will be subject to the rate limitations of paragraph 2 of Article 10 (Dividends).

Relation to Other Articles

Notwithstanding the foregoing limitations on source country taxation of royalties, the saving clause of paragraph 2 of Article 1 (Personal Scope) permits the United States to tax its residents and citizens, subject to the special foreign tax credit rules of paragraph 3 of Article 23 (Relief from Double Taxation), as if the Convention had not come into force.

As with other benefits of the Convention, the benefits of exclusive residence State taxation of royalties under paragraph 1 of Article 12, are available to a resident of the other State only if that resident is entitled to those benefits under the provisions of Article 22 (Limitation on Benefits).

Article 13 (Gains)

Article 13 assigns either primary or exclusive taxing jurisdiction over gains from the alienation of property to the State of residence or the State of source and defines the terms necessary to apply the Article.

Paragraph 1

Paragraph 1 of Article 13 preserves the non-exclusive right of the State of source to tax gains attributable to the alienation of real property situated in that State. The paragraph therefore permits the United States to apply section 897 of the Code to tax gains derived by a resident of the other Contracting State that are attributable to the alienation of real property situated in the United States (as defined in paragraph 2). Gains attributable to the alienation of real property include gain from any other property that is treated as a real property interest within the meaning of paragraph 2.

Paragraph 2

Paragraph 2 defines the term "real property situated in the other Contracting State." The term includes real property referred to in Article 6 (Income from Real Property) (i.e., interests in the real property itself) and certain other interests in such property. Such other interests include shares or other comparable interests in a company that is (or is treated as) a resident of the source State, the assets of which company consist wholly or principally of real property situated in the source State. In addition, interests in a partnership, trust, or estate, to the extent that the assets of such entity consist of real property situated in the source State, are included in this definition.

Finally, paragraph 2 provides that, with respect to the United States, the term "real property situated in the other State" includes a United States real property interest, as that term is defined in the Internal Revenue Code as amended (without changing the general principles thereof). Under section 897(c) of the Code the term "United States real property interest" includes shares in a U.S. corporation that owns sufficient U.S. real property interests to satisfy an asset-ratio test on certain testing dates. The term also includes certain foreign corporations that have elected to be treated as U.S. corporations for this purpose. Section 897(i).

Thus, the United States preserves its right to collect the tax imposed by section 897 of the Code on gains derived by foreign persons from the disposition of United States real property interests. The reference in paragraph 1 to gains "attributable to" the alienation of real property is intended to confirm that the U.S. taxing right extends to gains arising from indirect dispositions described in section 897(g). Moreover, in applying paragraph 1 the United States will look through distributions made by a REIT. Accordingly, distributions made by a REIT are taxable under paragraph 1 of Article 13 (not under Article 10 (Dividends)) when they are attributable to gains derived from the alienation of real property.

Paragraph 3

Paragraph 3 of Article 13 deals with the taxation of certain gains from the alienation of movable property forming part of the business property of a permanent establishment that an enterprise of a Contracting State has in the other Contracting State or of movable property pertaining to a fixed base available to a resident of a Contracting State in the other Contracting State for the purpose of performing independent personal services. This also includes gains from the alienation of such a permanent establishment (alone or with the whole enterprise) or of such fixed base. Such gains may be taxed in the State in which the permanent establishment or fixed base is located.

A resident of the other Contracting State that is a partner in a partnership doing business in the United States generally will have a permanent establishment in the United States as a result of the activities of the partnership, assuming that the activities of the partnership rise to the level of a permanent establishment. Rev. Rul. 91-32, 1991-1 C.B. 107. Accordingly, under paragraph 3, the United States generally may tax a partner's distributive share of income realized by a partnership on the disposition of movable property forming part of the business property of the partnership in the United States.

The rule in paragraph 3 of Article 28 (Miscellaneous) dealing with deferred income and expenses of a permanent establishment or fixed base applies to paragraph 3 of this Article. Thus, gain that is attributable to a permanent establishment or fixed base, but is deferred until after the permanent establishment or fixed base no longer exists, may nevertheless be taxed by the State in which the permanent establishment or fixed base was located.

Paragraph 4

Paragraph 4 limits the taxing jurisdiction of the state of source with respect to gain from the alienation of ships and aircraft operated in international traffic. Under this paragraph, when such income is derived by an enterprise of a Contracting State it is taxable only in that Contracting State. Notwithstanding paragraph 3, the rules of this paragraph apply even if the income is attributable to a permanent establishment maintained by the enterprise in the other Contracting State. This result is consistent with the general rule under Article 8 (Shipping and Air Transport) that confers exclusive taxing rights over international shipping and air transport income on the state of residence of the enterprise deriving such income.

Paragraph 4 of Article 13 also provides that gains described in Article 12 (Royalties) shall be taxable in accordance with the provisions of Article 12. This paragraph applies to gains derived from the alienation of rights to intangible property if the amount of the gain is contingent on the productivity, use of disposition thereof, which are described in paragraph 2 of Article 12.

Paragraph 5

Paragraph 5 of Article 13 grants to the State of residence of the alienator the exclusive right to tax gains from the alienation of property other than those specifically referred to in paragraphs 1 through 4. For example, gain derived from shares, other than shares described in paragraphs 2 or 3, debt instruments and various financial instruments, may be taxed only in the State of residence, to the extent such income is not otherwise characterized as income taxable under another article (e.g., Article 10 (Dividends) or Article 11 (Interest)). Similarly, gain derived from the alienation of tangible personal property, other than tangible personal property described in paragraph 3, may be taxed only in the State of residence of the alienator. As noted above, gain derived from the alienation of any property, such as a patent or copyright, that produces income taxable under Article 12 (Royalties) is taxable under Article 12 and not under this Article, provided that such gain is of the type described in paragraph 2(b) of Article 12 (i.e., it is contingent on the productivity, use, or disposition of the property). Thus, under either Article such gain is taxable only in the State of residence of the alienator.

Paragraph 6

Both paragraph 6 and paragraph 7 provide rules intended to coordinate the timing of the recognition of income under the U.S. and Swiss tax systems.

Paragraph 6 provides authority for coordination of Swiss and U.S. rules with respect to the nonrecognition of gain on corporate organizations, reorganizations, mergers, or similar transactions. Where a resident of one of the Contracting States alienates property in such a transaction, and profit, gain or income with respect to such alienation is not recognized for income tax purposes in the Contracting State of residence, the competent authority of the other State may agree, pursuant to paragraph 6, if requested by the person acquiring the property, to defer the recognition of the profit, gain or income with respect to such property. This deferral shall be for such time and under such conditions as may be stipulated in the agreement.

One situation in which this provision might be useful is the merger of two companies that are resident in one Contracting State, both of which have permanent establishments in the other Contracting State. For example, if two U.S. resident corporations, each with a permanent establishment in Switzerland, merged in a transaction that qualified as a tax-free reorganization under section 368 but was taxable in Switzerland, Switzerland could tax built-in gain on assets of the permanent establishments. When those assets eventually were sold, the United States might also tax the gain, but without a foreign tax credit if the period for tax credit carryovers had already run. In that case, the company surviving the merger could request that the Swiss competent authority defer recognition of the gain until actual disposition of the assets, in order to assure a U.S. foreign tax credit for the Swiss tax. Whether deferral should be granted is a matter entirely within the discretion of the competent authority.

Paragraph 7

Paragraph 7 provides a rule to coordinate U.S. and Swiss taxation of gains in circumstances where a resident of one of the Contracting States is subject to tax in both Contracting States and one Contracting State deems a taxable alienation of property by such resident to have occurred, while the other Contracting State at that time does not find a realization, recognition or inclusion of income and thus defers, but does not forgive, taxation. In such a case the resident may elect in the annual return of income for the year of such alienation to be liable to tax in the latter Contracting State as if he had sold and repurchased the property for an amount equal to its fair market value at a time immediately prior to the deemed alienation. This provision might be useful in a case where a U.S. corporation transfers assets from a permanent establishment in Switzerland to its home office in the United States. Switzerland generally would tax any built-in gain upon the transfer, but the United States would defer taxation until the property actually was sold. If the period for foreign tax credit carryovers had already run, the U.S. corporation might not receive a foreign tax credit, resulting in double taxation. If the U.S. corporation elected the benefits of paragraph 7, it would be subject to U.S. tax currently on the built-in gain, and take a new tax basis in the property.

Unlike paragraph 6, paragraph 7 is self-executing and does not require the agreement of the relevant competent authority. However, if in one Contracting State there are losses and gains from deemed alienation of different properties, then paragraph 7 must be applied consistently in the other Contracting State within the taxable period with respect to all such properties. Paragraph 7 only applies, however, if the deemed alienation of the properties results in a net gain.

Relation to Other Articles

Notwithstanding the foregoing limitations on source country taxation of certain gains, the saving clause of paragraph 2 of Article 1 (Personal Scope) generally permits the United States to tax gains realized by its residents and citizens, subject to the special rules of Article 23 (Relief from Double Taxation), as if the Convention had not come into effect. Thus, except as described below, the limitations in this Article on the right of the United States to tax gains do not apply to gains of a U.S. citizen or resident.

The saving clause of paragraph 2 of Article 1 (Personal Scope) does not apply to paragraphs 6 or 7 of Article 13 by reason of paragraph 3(a) of Article 1. Thus, a U.S. citizen resident in Switzerland may, subject to the discretion of the U.S. competent authority, obtain relief under paragraph 6 in the form of deferred recognition of profit, gain, or income that is otherwise recognized or included in income under the Code but not under Swiss law. Under Article 7, a U.S. corporation that is subject to tax upon a transfer of property from its Swiss permanent establishment to its U.S. head office may elect to be subject to tax in the United States on the built-in gain and receive a step-up in basis for U.S. tax purposes.

The benefits of Article 13 are also subject to the provisions of Article 22 (Limitation on Benefits). Thus, only a resident of a Contracting State that satisfies one of the conditions in Article 22 is entitled to the benefits of this Article.

Article 14 (Independent Personal Services)

The Convention deals in separate articles with different classes of income from personal services. Article 14 deals with the general class of income from independent personal services and Article 15 deals with the general class of income from dependent personal service. Articles 16 through 20 provide exceptions or additions to these general rules for directors' fees (Article 16); performance income of artistes and sportsmen (Article 17); pensions and annuities (Article 18); government service salaries and pensions, and social security benefits (Article 19); and certain income of students and trainees (Article 20).

Paragraph 1

Paragraph 1 of Article 14 provides the general rule that an individual who is a resident of a Contracting State and who derives income from the performance of personal services of an independent character will be exempt from tax in respect of that income by the other Contracting State unless certain conditions are satisfied. The income may be taxed in the other Contracting State only if the services are performed there and the income is attributable to a fixed base that is regularly available to the individual in that other State for the purpose of performing his services.

Income derived by persons other than individuals or groups of individuals from the performance of independent personal services is not covered by Article 14. Such income generally would be business profits taxable in accordance with Article 7 (Business Profits). Income derived by employees of such persons generally would be taxable in accordance with Article 15 (Dependent Personal Services).

The term "fixed base" is not defined in the Convention, but its meaning is understood to be similar, but not identical, to that of the term "permanent establishment," as defined in Article 5 (Permanent Establishment). For example, while it is appropriate in some cases to apply the rules in paragraphs 2 through 6 to determine whether an individual has a fixed base (see Rev. Rul. 75-131, 1975-1 C.B. 389), the rule of paragraph 7 of Article 5 concerning subsidiaries does not apply.

The term "regularly available" also is not defined in the Convention. Whether a fixed base is regularly available to a person will be determined based on all the facts and circumstances. In general, however, the term encompasses situations where a fixed base is at the disposal of the individual whenever he performs services in that State. It is not necessary that the individual regularly use the fixed base, only that the fixed base be regularly available to him. For example, a U.S. resident individual who is a partner in a law firm that has offices in Switzerland would be considered to have a fixed base regularly available to him in Switzerland if the law firm had an office in Switzerland that was available to him whenever he wished to conduct business there, regardless of how frequently he used the office, or if, in fact, he used it at all. Thus, the fixed base will be considered to be regularly available to him regardless of whether he conducts his activities there. On the other hand, a U.S. resident individual who had no office in Switzerland and occasionally rented a hotel room there to serve as a temporary office would not be considered to have a fixed base regularly available to him.

The taxing right conferred by this Article with respect to income from independent personal services is somewhat more limited than that provided in Article 7 for the taxation of business profits. In both articles the income of a resident of one Contracting State must be attributable to a permanent establishment or fixed base in the other in order for that other State to have a taxing right. In Article 14 the income also must be attributable to services performed in that other State, while Article 7 does not require that all of the income-generating activities be performed in the State where the permanent establishment is located.

The term "personal services of an independent character" is not defined in the Convention. It clearly includes those activities listed in paragraph 2 of Article 14 of the OECD Model, such as independent scientific, literary, artistic, educational or teaching activities, as well as the independent activities of physicians, lawyers, engineers, architects, dentists, and accountants. The OECD list, however, is not exhaustive. The term includes all personal services performed by an individual for his own account, whether as a sole proprietor or as a partner, where he receives the income and bears the risk of loss arising from performing the services. The taxation of income of an individual from those types of independent services described in Articles 16 through 20 is governed by the provisions of those articles. For example, taxation of the income of a professional musician would be governed by Article 17 (Artistes and Sportsmen) rather than Article 14.

This Article applies to income derived by a partner resident in the Contracting State that is attributable to personal services of an independent character performed in the other State through a partnership that has a fixed base in that other Contracting State. Income which may be taxed under this Article includes all income attributable to the fixed base in respect of the performance of the personal services carried on by the partnership (whether by the partner himself, other partners in the partnership, or by employees assisting the partners) and any income from activities ancillary to the performance of those services (for example, charges for facsimile services). Income that is not derived from the performance of personal services and that is not ancillary thereto (for example, rental income from subletting office space), will be governed by other Articles of the Convention.

The application of Article 14 to a service partnership may be illustrated by the following example: a partnership formed in the Contracting State has five partners (who agree to split profits equally), four of whom are resident and perform personal services only in the Contracting State at Office A, and one of whom performs personal services from Office B, a fixed base in the other State. In this case, the four partners of the partnership resident in the Contracting State may be taxed in the other State in respect of their share of the income attributable to the fixed base, Office B. The services giving rise to income which may be attributed to the fixed base would include not only the services performed by the one resident partner, but also, for example, if one of the four other partners came to the other State and worked on an Office B matter there, the income in respect of those services also. As noted above, this would be the case regardless of whether the partner from the Contracting State actually visited or used Office B when performing services in the other State.

Paragraph 3 of Article 28 (Miscellaneous) refers to Article 14. That rule clarifies that income and expense that is attributable to a fixed base, but that is deferred until after the fixed base no longer exists or is no longer available to the person who performed the services may nevertheless be taxed or deducted, as the case may be, in the State in which the fixed base was located. Thus, under Article 14, income derived by an individual resident of a Contracting State from services performed in the other Contracting State and attributable to a fixed base there may be taxed by that other State even if the income is deferred and received after there is no longer a fixed base available to the resident in that other State.

Income from services in which capital is a material income producing factor will, however, generally be governed by the provisions of Article 7 (Business Profits). As noted below in the discussion of paragraph 2 of the Article, however, the result should be essentially the same whether the income is subject to the rules of Article 7 or 14.

Paragraph 2

This paragraph incorporates the principles of Article 7 into Article 14. Thus, all relevant expenses, wherever incurred, must be allowed as deductions in computing the net income from services subject to tax in the Contracting State in which the fixed base is located.

Relation to other Articles

Article 14 is subject to the saving clause of paragraph 4 of Article 1 (Personal Scope). Thus, if an individual resident of Switzerland who is also a U.S. citizen performs independent personal services in the United States, the United States may tax his income without regard to the restrictions of this Article, subject to the special foreign tax credit rules of paragraph 3 of Article 23 (Relief from Double Taxation).

Article 15 (Dependent Personal Services)

Article 15 assigns taxing jurisdiction over remuneration derived by a resident of a Contracting State as an employee between the States of source and residence.

Paragraph 1

The general rule of Article 15 is contained in paragraph 1. Remuneration derived by a resident of a Contracting State as an employee may be taxed by the State of residence, and the remuneration also may be taxed by that other Contracting State to the extent derived from employment exercised (i.e., services performed) in the other Contracting State. Paragraph 1 also provides that the more specific rules of Article 16 (Directors' Fees), 18 (Pensions and Annuities) and 19 (Government Service and Social Security) apply in the case of employment income described in one of those articles. Thus, even though the State of source has a right to tax employment income under Article 15, it may not have the right to tax that income under the Convention if the income is described, e.g., in Article 18 (Pensions and Annuities), and is not taxable in the State of source under the provisions of that article.

Consistent with the rule of paragraph 3 of Article 28 (Miscellaneous), which is based on Code section 864(c)(6), Article 15 also applies regardless of the timing of actual payment for services. Thus, a bonus paid with respect to services performed in a Contracting State in a particular taxable year would be subject to Article 15 for that year even if it was paid after the close of the year. Similarly, an annuity received for services performed in a taxable year would be subject to Article 15 despite the fact that it was paid in subsequent years. In either case, whether such payments were taxable in the State where the employment was exercised would depend on whether the tests of paragraph 2 of Article 15 were satisfied.

Paragraph 2

Paragraph 2 sets forth an exception to the general rule that employment income may be taxed in the State where the employment is exercised. Under paragraph 2, the State where the employment is exercised may not tax the income from the employment if three conditions are satisfied: (1) the individual is present in that State for a period or periods not exceeding 183 days in any twelve month period that begins or ends during the relevant calendar year; (2) the remuneration is paid by, or on behalf of, an employer who is not a resident of that Contracting

State; and (3) the remuneration is not borne as a deductible expense by a permanent establishment or fixed base that the employer has in that State. In order for the remuneration to be exempt from tax in the source State, all three conditions must be satisfied. This exception is identical to that set forth in the OECD Model.

The 183-day period in condition (a) is to be measured using the "days of physical presence" method. Under this method, the days that are counted include any day in which a part of the day is spent in the host country. (Rev. Rul. 56-24, 1956-1 C.B. 851.) Thus, days that are counted include the days of arrival and departure; weekends and holidays on which the employee does not work but is present within the country; vacation days spent in the country before, during or after the employment period, unless the individual's presence before or after the employment can be shown to be independent of his presence there for employment purposes; and time during periods of sickness, training periods, strikes, etc., when the individual is present but not working. If illness prevented the individual from leaving the country in sufficient time to qualify for the benefit, those days will not count. Also, any part of a day spend in the host country while in transit between two points outside the host country is not counted. These rules are consistent with the description of the 183-day period in paragraph 5 of the Commentary to Article 15 in the OECD Model.

Conditions (b) and (c) are intended to ensure that a Contracting State will not be required to allow a deduction to the payor for compensation paid and at the same time to exempt the employee on the amount received. Accordingly, if a foreign person pays the salary of an employee, but a host country corporation or permanent establishment reimburses the payor with a payment that can be identified as a reimbursement, either condition (b) or (c), as the case may be, will be considered not to have been fulfilled.

The references to remuneration "borne by" a permanent establishment or fixed base is understood to encompass all expenses that economically are incurred and not merely expenses that are currently deductible for tax purposes. Accordingly, the expenses referred to include expenses that are capitalizable as well as those that are currently deductible. Further, salaries paid by residents that are exempt from income taxation may be considered to be borne by a permanent establishment or fixed base notwithstanding the fact that the expenses will be neither deductible nor capitalizable since the payor is exempt from tax.

In many cases, it may not be possible to know until year-end whether a person providing independent personal services has met the 183-day threshold with respect to a Contracting State, nothing in the Convention precludes that State from withholding tax during the year and refunding after the close of the year if the taxability threshold has not been met. This is made explicit in Paragraph 3 of the Memorandum of Understanding, which further provides that the taxpayer will receive such a refund only if the claim for refund is filed with the relevant tax authority within five years after the close of the calendar year in which the tax is withheld.

Paragraph 3

Paragraph 3 contains a special rule applicable to remuneration for services performed by a resident of a Contracting State as an employee aboard a ship or aircraft operated in international traffic. Such remuneration may be taxed only in the State of residence of the employee if the services are performed as a member of the regular complement of the ship or aircraft. The "regular complement" includes the crew. In the case of a cruise ship, it may also include others, such as entertainers, lecturers, etc., employed by the shipping company to serve on the ship throughout its voyage. The use of the term "regular complement" is intended to clarify that a person who exercises his employment as, for example, an insurance salesman while aboard a ship or aircraft is not covered by this paragraph. This paragraph is inapplicable to persons dealt with in Article 14 (Independent Personal Services).

The comparable paragraph in the OECD Model provides that such income may be taxed (on a non-exclusive basis) in the Contracting State in which the place of effective management of the employing enterprise is situated. This rule has not been adopted by the United States because the United States exercises its taxing jurisdiction over an employee only if the employee is a U.S. citizen or resident, or the services are performed by the employee in the United States. Tax cannot be imposed simply because an employee works for an enterprise that is a resident of the United States. The rule in the Convention, which is the same as the U.S. Model, ensures that, given U.S. law, each employee will be subject to one level of tax.

Relation to Other Articles

If a U.S. citizen who is resident in the other Contracting State performs services as an employee in the United States and meets the conditions of paragraph 2 for source country exemption, he nevertheless is taxable in the United States by virtue of the saving clause of paragraph 4 of Article 1 (General Scope), subject to the special foreign tax credit rule of paragraph 3 of Article 23 (Relief from Double Taxation).

Article 16 (Directors' Fees)

This Article provides that a Contracting State may tax the fees or other remuneration paid by a company that is a resident of that State for services performed by a resident of the other State in his capacity as a director of the company. The State of residence of the company may tax all of the remuneration, without regard to where the services are performed. This rule is an exception to the more general rules of Article 14 (Independent Personal Services) and Article 15 (Dependent Personal Services). Thus, for example, in determining whether a director's fee paid to a non-employee director is subject to tax in the country of residence of the company, it is not relevant to establish whether the fee is attributable to a fixed base in the State.

The provision in the Convention is identical to the analogous provision in the OECD Model. The U.S. Model reaches a different result, providing that the State of residence of the company may tax nonresident directors with no time or dollar threshold, but only with respect to remuneration for services performed in that State.

Because this Article does not restrict taxation by either Contracting State, the saving clause of paragraph 2 of the Article 1 (Personal Scope) is irrelevant. If a U.S. citizen who is a Swiss resident is a director of a Swiss corporation, the United States may tax his full remuneration for those services, subject, however, to the special provisions of paragraph 3 of Article 23 (Relief from Double Taxation).

Article 17 (Artistes and Sportsmen)

This Article deals with the taxation in a Contracting State of artistes (i.e., performing artists and entertainers) and sportsmen resident in the other Contracting State from the performance of their services as such. The Article applies both to the income of an entertainer or sportsman who performs services on his own behalf and one who performs his services on behalf of another person, either as an employee of that person, or pursuant to any other arrangement. The rules of this Article take precedence, in some circumstances, over those of Articles 14 (Independent Personal Services) and 15 (Dependent Personal Services).

This Article applies only with respect to the income of performing artists and sportsmen. Others involved in a performance or athletic event, such as producers, directors, technicians, managers, coaches, etc., remain subject to the provisions of Articles 14 and 15. In addition, except as provided in paragraph 2, income earned by juridical persons is not covered by Article 17.

Paragraph 1

Paragraph 1 describes the circumstances in which a Contracting State may tax the performance income of an entertainer or sportsman who is a resident of the other Contracting State. Under the paragraph, income derived by an individual resident of a Contracting State from activities as an entertainer or sportsman exercised in the other Contracting State may be taxed in that other State if the amount of the gross receipts derived by the performer exceeds $10,000 (or its equivalent in Swiss francs) for the taxable year. The $10,000 includes expenses reimbursed to the individual or borne on his behalf. If the gross receipts exceed $10,000, the full amount, not just the excess, may be taxed in the State of performance.

The OECD Model provides for taxation by the country of performance of the remuneration of entertainers or sportsmen with no dollar or time threshold. The United States introduces the dollar threshold test in its treaties to distinguish between two groups of entertainers and sportsmen -- those who are paid very large sums of money for very short periods of service, and who would, therefore, normally be exempt from host country tax under the standard personal services income rules, and those who earn relatively modest amounts and are, therefore, not easily distinguishable from those who earn other types of personal service income. The United States has entered a reservation to the OECD Model on this point.

Tax may be imposed under paragraph 1 even if the performer would have been exempt from tax under Articles 14 (Independent Personal Services) or 15 (Dependent Personal Services). On the other hand, if the performer would be exempt from host-country tax under Article 17, but would be taxable under either Article 14 or 15, tax may be imposed under either of those Articles. Thus, for example, if a performer derives remuneration from his activities in an independent capacity, and the remuneration is not attributable to a fixed base, he may be taxed by the host State in accordance with Article 17 if his remuneration exceeds $10,000 annually, despite the fact that he generally would be exempt from host State taxation under Article 14. However, a performer who receives less than the $10,000 threshold amount and therefore is not taxable under Article 17, nevertheless may be subject to tax in the host country under Articles 14 or 15 if the tests for host-country taxability under those Articles are met. For example, if an entertainer who is an independent contractor earns $9,000 of income in a State for the calendar year, but the income is attributable to a fixed base regularly available to him in the State of performance, that State may tax his income under Article 14. This interpretation is consistent with the result under the U.S. Model, which spells out the relationship between the Articles in more detail than the Convention or the OECD Model, but does not require a Contracting State to prove that the income would have been exempt under Article 14 or 15 before applying the provisions of Article 17.

Since it frequently is not possible to know until year-end whether the income an entertainer or sportsman derived from performing in a Contracting State will exceed $10,000, nothing in the Convention precludes that State from withholding tax during the year and refunding after the close of the year if the taxability threshold has not been met. This is made explicit in Paragraph 3 of the Memorandum of Understanding, which further provides that the taxpayer will receive such a refund only if the claim for refund is filed with the relevant tax authority within five years after the close of the calendar year in which the tax is withheld.

As explained in paragraph 9 of the OECD Commentaries to Article 17, Article 17 applies to all income connected with a performance by an entertainer, such as appearance fees, award or prize money, and a share of the gate receipts. Income derived from a Contracting State by a performer who is a resident of the other Contracting State from other than actual performance, such as royalties from record sales and payments for product endorsements, is not covered by this Article, but by other articles of the Convention, as appropriate, such as Article 12 (Royalties) or Article 14 (Independent Personal Services). For example, if an entertainer receives royalty income from the sale of live recordings, the royalty income would be exempt from source country tax under Article 12, even if the performance was conducted in the source country, although he could be taxed in the source country with respect to income from the performance itself under this Article if the dollar threshold is exceeded.

In determining whether income falls under Article 17 or another article, the controlling factor will be whether the income in question is predominantly attributable to the performance itself or other activities or property rights. For instance, a fee paid to a performer for endorsement of a performance in which the performer will participate would be considered to be so closely associated with the performance itself that it normally would fall within Article 17. Similarly, a sponsorship fee paid by a business in return for the right to attach its name to the performance would be so closely associated with the performance that it would fall under Article 17 as well. A cancellation fee would not be considered to fall within Article 17 but would be other income within the meaning of Article 21 (Other Income). Each case must be evaluated based on its individual facts and circumstances.

As indicated in paragraph 4 of the Commentaries to Article 17 of the OECD Model, where an individual fulfills a dual role as performer and non-performer (such as a player-coach or an actor-director), but his role in one of the two capacities is negligible, the predominant character of the individual's activities should control the characterization of those activities. In other cases, there should be an apportionment between the performance-related compensation and other compensation.

Paragraph 2

Paragraph 2 is intended to deal with the potential for abuse when a performer's income does not accrue directly to the performer himself, but to another person. Foreign performers commonly perform in the United States as employees of, or under contract with, a company or other person.

The relationship may truly be one of employee and employer, with no abuse of the tax system either intended or realized. On the other hand, the "employer" may, for example, be a company established and owned by the performer, which is merely acting as the nominal income recipient in respect of the remuneration for the entertainer's performance (a "star company"). The performer may act as an "employee", receive a modest salary, and arrange to receive the remainder of the income from his performance in another form or at a later time. In such case, absent the provisions of paragraph 2, the income arguably could escape host-country tax because the company earns business profits but has no permanent establishment in that country. The performer may largely or entirely escape host-country tax by receiving only a small salary in the year the services are performed, perhaps small enough to place him below the dollar threshold in paragraph 1. The performer might arrange to receive further payments in a later year, when he is not subject to host-country tax, perhaps as deferred salary payments, dividends or liquidating distributions.

Paragraph 2 seeks to prevent this type of abuse while at the same time protecting taxpayers' rights to the benefits of the Convention when there is a legitimate employee-employer relationship between the performer and the person providing his services. Under paragraph 2, when the income accrues to a person other than the performer, and the performer or related persons participate, directly or indirectly, in the receipts or profits of that other person, the income may be taxed in the Contracting State where the performer's services are exercised, without regard to the provisions of the Convention concerning business profits (Article 7) or independent personal services (Article 14). Thus, even if the "employer" has no permanent establishment or fixed base in the host country, its income may be subject to tax there under the provisions of paragraph 2. Taxation under paragraph 2 is on the person providing the services of the performer. This paragraph does not affect the rules of paragraph 1, which apply to the performer himself. The income taxable by virtue of paragraph 2 is reduced to the extent of salary payments to the performer, which fall under paragraph 1.

For purposes of paragraph 2, income is deemed to accrue to another person (i.e., the person providing the services of the performer) if that other person has control over, or the right to receive, gross income in respect of the services of the entertainer or sportsman. Direct or indirect participation in the profits of a person may include, but is not limited to, the accrual or receipt of deferred remuneration, bonuses, fees, dividends, partnership income or other income or distributions.

Paragraph 2 does not apply if it is established that neither the performer nor any persons related to the performer participate directly or indirectly in the receipts or profits of the person providing the services of the performer. Assume, for example, that a circus owned by a U.S. corporation performs in Switzerland, and promoters of the performance in Switzerland pay the circus, which, in turn, pays salaries to the circus performers. The circus is determined to have no permanent establishment in Switzerland. Since the circus performers do not participate in the profits of the circus, but merely receive their salaries out of the circus' gross receipts, the circus is protected by Article 7 and its income is not subject to host-country tax. Whether the salaries of the circus performers are subject to host-country tax depends on whether they exceed the $10,000 threshold in paragraph 1, and, if not, whether they are taxable under Article 15 (Dependent Personal Services).

Since pursuant to Article 1 (Personal Scope) the Convention only applies to persons who are residents of one of the Contracting States, if the star company is not a resident of one of the Contracting States then taxation of the income is not affected by Article 17 or any other provision of the Convention.

This exception from paragraph 2 for non-abusive cases is not found in the OECD Model. The United States has entered a reservation to the OECD Model on this point.

Relationship to other Articles

This Article is subject to the provisions of the saving clause of paragraph 2 of Article 1 (Personal Scope). Thus, if an entertainer or sportsman who is resident in Switzerland is a citizen of the United States, the United States may tax all of his income from performances in the United

States without regard to the provisions of this Article, subject, however, to the special provisions of paragraph 3 of Article 23 (Relief from Double Taxation).

Article 18 (Pensions and Annuities)

This Article deals with the taxation of private (i.e., non-government) pensions, annuities, and similar benefits.

Unlike most U.S. tax treaties, the Convention contains no rules for alimony and child support payments. As a result, alimony and child support payments fall under the rule for "other income" in paragraph 1 of Article 21 (Other Income) and may be taxed only in the country of residence of the recipient.

Paragraph 1

Paragraph 1 provides that private pensions and other similar remuneration derived and beneficially owned by a resident of a Contracting State in consideration of past employment are taxable only in the State of residence of the recipient. Although the Convention does not make explicit the fact that the term "pensions and other similar remuneration" includes both periodic and lump-sum payments, it is understood that this would be the case under the domestic law of both Contracting States. Treatment of such payments under the prior Convention is essentially the same as under the Convention, except that the rules of the prior Convention apply only to periodic payments. The term "pensions and other similar remuneration" includes amounts paid by all private retirement plans and arrangements in consideration of past employment, regardless of whether they are qualified plans under U.S. law, including plans and arrangements described in section 457 or 414(d) of the Internal Revenue Code. It also includes an Individual Retirement Account.

Pensions in respect of government service are not covered by this paragraph. They are covered either by paragraph 2 of Article 19 (Government Service and Social Security) or, if they are in the form of social security benefits, paragraph 4 of Article 19.

Paragraph 2

Under paragraph 2, annuities that are derived and beneficially owned by a resident of a Contracting State are taxable only in that State.

An "annuity," as the term is used in paragraph 2, means a stated sum paid periodically at stated times or during a specified number of years or for life under an obligation to make the payment in return for adequate and full consideration (other than for services rendered). An annuity received in considerations for services rendered would be treated as deferred compensation and generally taxable in accordance with Article 15 (Dependent Personal Services).

The provisions of this Article are subject to the saving clause of paragraph 2 of Article 1 (Personal Scope). Thus, a U.S. citizen who is a resident of Switzerland and receives a pension or annuity from the United States may be subject to U.S. tax on the payment, notwithstanding the rules in Article 18 that give the State of residence of the recipient the exclusive taxing right.

Article 19 (Government Service and Social Security)

This Article deals with the taxation of income (including pensions) from governmental employment and social security benefits.

Paragraph 1

Subparagraphs (a) and (b) of paragraph 1 deal with the taxation of government compensation (other than a pension addressed in paragraph 2). Subparagraph 1(a) provides that remuneration paid by one of the Contracting States or by its political subdivisions or local authorities to any individual who is rendering services to that State, political subdivision or local authority is exempt from tax by the other State. Under paragraph 1(b), such payments are, however, taxable exclusively in the other State (i.e., the host State) if the services are rendered in that other State and the individual is a resident of that State who is either a national of that State or a person who did not become resident in that State solely for purposes of rendering the services. This paragraph follows the OECD Model, but differs from the U.S. Model, in applying only to government employees and not to independent contractors engaged by governments to perform services for them.

Paragraph 2

Paragraph 2 deals with the taxation of a pension paid by, or out of funds created by, one of the States or a political subdivision or a local authority thereof to an individual in respect of services rendered to that State or subdivision or authority. Subparagraph 2(a) provides that such a pension is taxable only in that State. Subparagraph 2(b) provides an exception under which such a pension is taxable only in the other State if the individual is a resident of, and a national of, that other State. Pensions paid to retired civilian and military employees of a government of either State are intended to be covered under paragraph 2. When benefits paid by a State in respect of services rendered to that State or subdivision or authority are in the form of social security benefits, however, those payments are covered by paragraph 4.

Paragraph 3

Paragraph 3 provides that the provisions of Articles 15 (Dependent Personal Services), 16 (Directors' Fees), and 18 (Pensions and Annuities) shall apply to remuneration and pensions in respect of services rendered in connection with a business carried on by one of the States or a political subdivision or a local authority thereof. This treatment is consistent with the U.S. and OECD Models, since the OECD Model excludes payments in respect of services rendered in connection with a business carried on by the governmental entity paying the compensation or pension and the U.S. Model excludes services that do not relate to the discharge of governmental functions.

Paragraph 4

The treatment of social security payments and other public pensions is dealt with in paragraph 4. This paragraph provides that, notwithstanding the provisions of Article 18 (Pensions and Annuities) under which private pensions are taxable exclusively in the State of residence of the beneficial owner, payments made by one of the Contracting States under the provisions of its social security legislation and other public pensions to a resident of the other Contracting State or to a citizen of the United States may be taxed in both Contracting States. However, several rules in Articles 18 and 23 (Relief from Double Taxation) limit the likelihood of double taxation.

The treatment of social security and other public pension benefits in the Convention differs from that in the U.S. Model, under which the source State retains exclusive taxing rights. This treatment is necessary in order to avoid the double taxation of U.S. social security benefits and other public pension benefits received by Swiss residents that would otherwise occur under the taxing systems of both countries. The United States, as the source country in this situation, subjects up to 85 percent of the benefits paid to U.S. citizens and nonresident aliens resident in Switzerland to taxation. Switzerland, as the residence country, subjects the U.S. benefits received by those individuals to taxation without providing any tax credit for the U.S. taxes paid. Switzerland is unable to provide a credit in these circumstances, even by treaty. Thus, those persons are subject to a substantial double tax burden. (No special double taxation relief rule is required in the reverse situation where Swiss social security benefits are paid to U.S. residents because Switzerland does not tax the benefits when it is the source country. If, in the future, Switzerland were to impose tax on such payments, a U.S. foreign tax credit would be available under the general provisions of paragraph 2 of Article 23.)

Under paragraph 4, the United States will limit its taxation of social security and other public pensions paid to Swiss residents to 15 percent of the gross payment. Further, paragraph 1(d) of Article 23 (Relief from Double Taxation) provides that Swiss residents subject to U.S. taxation of benefits under paragraph 4 of this article will receive a deduction from Swiss taxable income of an amount equal to the tax levied in the United States on the benefits, plus an exemption of one-third of the net amount of such payment. Double taxation of the benefits will, thus, be mitigated. For example, a U.S. social security payment of $100 to a Swiss resident, not a

U.S. citizen, will be subject to a U.S. tax of $15. Switzerland will tax only $56.70 of the benefits ($100 minus $15 minus $28.30 (one-third of $85.00)). Assuming a Swiss tax rate of 25%, the Swiss tax will be $14.80, for a total tax burden of $29.80.

This paragraph applies to social security beneficiaries whether they have contributed to the system as private sector or government employees. As noted in paragraph 6 of the Protocol, the phrase "other public pensions" is intended to refer to United States tier 1 Railroad Retirement benefits. Unlike the U.S. Model, this paragraph of the Convention does not refer to U.S. citizens, because U.S. residence-basis taxation of Swiss social security benefits is not limited by the Convention.

Relation to Other Articles

Under paragraph 3(b) of Article 1 (Personal Scope), the saving clause (paragraph 2 of Article 1) does not apply to the benefits conferred by one of the States under paragraphs 1 and 2 of Article 19 if the recipient of the benefits is neither a citizen of that State, nor a person who has immigrant status there (i.e., in the United States, a "green card" holder). Thus, for example, an individual who is resident in the United States and receives a pension paid by Switzerland in respect of services rendered to the Government of Switzerland is taxable on this pension only in Switzerland unless the individual is a U.S. citizen or acquires a U.S. green card.

Paragraph 4 is subject to the saving clause of paragraph 2 of Article 1. Thus, the United States will not limit its tax on the social security benefits paid by the United States to a U.S. citizen who is a resident of Switzerland.

Article 20 (Students and Trainees)

Article 20 provides rules for host-country taxation of visiting students, apprentices and business trainees. Persons who meet the tests of the Article will be exempt from tax in the State that they are visiting with respect to designated classes of income. Several conditions must be satisfied in order for an individual to be entitled to the benefits of this Article.

First, the visitor must have been, either at the time of his arrival in the host State or immediately before, a resident of the other Contracting State. Second, the purpose of the visit must be the full-time education or training of the visitor. Thus, if the visitor comes principally to work in the host State but also is a part-time student, he would not be entitled to the benefits of this Article, even with respect to any payments he may receive from abroad for his maintenance or education, and regardless of whether or not he is in a degree program. Whether a student is considered full-time will be determined by the rules of the educational institutions at which he is studying. Similarly, a person who visits the host State for the purpose of obtaining business training and who also receives a salary from his employer for providing services would not be considered a trainee and would not be entitled to the benefits of this Article.

The host-country exemption in the Article applies only to payments received by the student, apprentice or business trainee for the purpose of his maintenance, education or training that arise outside the host State. A payment will be considered to arise outside the host State if the payor is located outside the host State. Thus, if an employer from one of the Contracting States sends an employee to the other Contracting State for training, the payments the trainee receives from abroad from his employer for his maintenance or training while he is present in the host State will be exempt from host-country tax. In all cases substance-over-form should prevail in determining the identity of the payor. Consequently, payments made directly or indirectly by the U.S. person with whom the visitor is training, but which have been routed through a non-host-country source, such as, for example, a foreign bank account, should not be treated as arising outside the United States for this purpose.

The saving clause of paragraph 2 of Article 1 (Personal Scope) does not apply to this Article with respect to an individual who is neither a citizen of the host State nor has been admitted for permanent residence there. The saving clause, however, does apply with respect to citizens and permanent residents of the host State. Thus, a U.S. citizen who is a resident of Switzerland and who visits the United States as a full-time student at a university will not be exempt from U.S. tax on remittances from abroad that otherwise constitute U.S. taxable income. A person, however, who is not a U.S. citizen, and who visits the United States as a student and remains long enough to become a resident under U.S. law, but does not become a permanent resident (i.e., does not acquire a green card), will be entitled to the full benefits of Article 20.

Article 21 (Other Income)

Article 21 generally assigns taxing jurisdiction over income not dealt with in the other articles (Articles 6 through 20) of the Convention to the state of residence of the beneficial owner of the income and defines the terms necessary to apply the article. An item of income is "dealt with" in an article if it is the type of income described in the article and it has its source in a Contracting State. For example, all royalty income that arises in a Contracting State is "dealt with" in Article 12 (Royalties), regardless of whether the beneficial owner of the income is a resident of a Contracting State.

Examples of items of income covered by Article 21 include punitive (but not compensatory) damages and income from various financial instruments to the extent derived by persons not engaged in the trade or business of dealing in such instruments (unless the transaction giving rise to the income is related to a trade or business, and therefore dealt with under Article 7). The article also applies to items of income that are not dealt with in the other articles because of their source or some other characteristic. For example, Article 11 (Interest) addresses only the taxation of interest arising in a Contracting State. Interest arising in a third State that is not attributable to a permanent establishment, therefore, is subject to Article 21.

Distributions from partnerships (in contrast to a distribution of income) and distributions from trusts are not generally dealt with under Article 21 because partnership and trust distributions generally do not constitute income. Under the Code, partners include in income their distributive share of partnership income annually, and partnership distributions themselves generally do not give rise to income. Also, under the Code, trust income and distributions have the character of the associated distributable net income and therefore would generally be covered by another article of the Convention. See Code section 641 et seq.

Paragraph 1

The general rule of Article 21 is contained in paragraph 1. Items of income not dealt with in other articles and beneficially owned by a resident of a Contracting State will be taxable only in the State of residence. This exclusive right of taxation applies irrespective of whether the residence State exercises its right to tax the income covered by the Article.

This paragraph differs in one respect from paragraph 1 in the U.S. Model, by referring to "items of income of a resident of a Contracting State" rather than "items of income beneficially owned by a resident of a Contracting State". The latter language, found in the U.S. Model, is not intended to effect a substantive change, but is merely to make explicit the implicit understanding in other treaties that have language similar to the Convention that the exclusive residence taxation provided by paragraph 1 applies only when a resident of a Contracting State is the beneficial owner of the income. Thus, source taxation of income not dealt with in other articles of the Convention is not limited by paragraph 1 if it is nominally paid to a resident of the other Contracting State, but is beneficially owned by a resident of a third State.

Paragraph 2

Paragraph 2 provides an exception to the general rule of paragraph 1 for income, other than income from real property, that is attributable to a permanent establishment or fixed base maintained in a Contracting State by a resident of the other Contracting State. The taxation of such income is governed by the provisions of Articles 7 (Business Profits) and 14 (Independent Personal Services). Therefore, income arising outside the United States that is attributable to a permanent establishment maintained in the United States by a resident of Switzerland generally would be taxable by the United States under the provisions of Article 7. This would be true whether the income is sourced in Switzerland or in a third State.

There is an exception to this general rule with respect to income from real property, as defined in paragraph 2 of Article 6 (Income from Real Property). If a Swiss resident derives income from real property located outside the United States (whether in Switzerland or in a third State) that is attributable to the resident's permanent establishment or fixed base in the United States, only Switzerland (i.e., the State of residence of the person deriving the income) and not the United States (i.e., the host State of the permanent establishment or fixed base) may tax that income. This special rule for foreign-situs real property is consistent with the general rule, also reflected in Article 6 (Income from Real Property), that only the situs and residence States may tax real property income. Even if such property is part of the property of a permanent establishment or fixed base in a Contracting State, that State may not tax if neither the situs of the property nor the residence of the owner is in that State.

Paragraph 3

Paragraph 3 provides that Article 21 does not apply to income subject to tax in either Contracting State on wagering, gambling, or lottery winnings. As a result, each Contracting State may tax those winnings under its domestic law, and will impose tax at source. The State in which the beneficial owner of the income is a resident will either provide a foreign tax credit for the source-country tax (in the case of the United States) or will exempt the income from tax (in the case of Switzerland). This rule is different from the rule under the U.S. and OECD Models, which treat gambling winnings as other income described in Article 21 and thus provide for exclusive taxation by the country of residence. This rule was included at the request of Switzerland.

Relation to Other Articles

This Article is subject to the saving clause of paragraph 2 of Article 1 (Personal Scope). Thus, the United States may tax the income of a Swiss resident that is not dealt with elsewhere in the Convention, if that Swiss resident is a citizen of the United States, subject, to the special provisions of paragraph 3 of Article 23 (Relief from Double Taxation). The Article is also subject to the provisions of Article 22 (Limitation on Benefits). Thus, if a resident of Switzerland earns income that falls within the scope of paragraph 1 of Article 21, but that is taxable by the United States under U.S. law, the income would be exempt from U.S. tax under the provisions of Article 21 only if the resident satisfies one of the tests of Article 22 for entitlement to benefits.

Article 22 (Limitation on Benefits)

Purpose of Limitation on Benefits Provisions

The United States views an income tax treaty as a vehicle for providing treaty benefits to residents of the two Contracting States. This statement begs the question of who is to be treated as a resident of a Contracting State for the purpose of being granted treaty benefits. The Commentaries to the OECD Model authorize a tax authority to deny benefits, under substance-over-form principles, to a nominee in one State deriving income from the other on behalf of a third-country resident. In addition, although the text of the OECD Model does not contain express anti-abuse provisions, the Commentaries to Article 1 contain an extensive discussion approving the use of such provisions in tax treaties in order to limit the ability of third state residents to obtain treaty benefits. The United States holds strongly to the view that tax treaties should include provisions that specifically prevent misuse of treaties by residents of third countries. Consequently, all recent U.S. income tax treaties contain comprehensive Limitation on Benefits provisions.

A treaty that provides treaty benefits to any resident of a Contracting State permits "treaty shopping": the use, by residents of third States, of legal entities established in a Contracting State with a principal purpose to obtain the benefits of a tax treaty between the United States and the other Contracting State. It is important to note that this definition of treaty shopping does not encompass every case in which a third state resident establishes an entity in a U.S. treaty partner, and that entity enjoys treaty benefits to which the third state resident would not itself be entitled. If the third country resident had substantial reasons for establishing the structure that were unrelated to obtaining treaty benefits, the structure would not fall within the definition of treaty shopping set forth above.

Of course, the fundamental problem presented by this approach is that it requires the tax administration to make a subjective determination of the taxpayer's intent. In order to avoid the administrative burdens of such an approach, Article 22 sets forth a series of mechanical tests. The assumption underlying each of these tests is that a taxpayer that satisfies the requirements of any of the tests probably has a real business purpose for the structure it has adopted, or has a sufficiently strong nexus to the other Contracting State (e.g., a resident individual) to warrant benefits even in the absence of a business connection, and that this business purpose or connection outweighs any purpose to obtain the benefits of the Convention.

For instance, the assumption underlying the active trade or business test under subparagraph 1(c) is that a third country resident that establishes a "substantial" operation in the other Contracting State and that derives income from a related activity in the United States would not do so primarily to avail itself of the benefits of the Convention; it is presumed in such a case that the investor had a valid business purpose for investing in the other Contracting State, and that the link between that trade or business and the U.S. activity that generates the treaty-benefitted income manifests a business purpose for placing the U.S. investments in the entity in the other State. It is considered unlikely that the investor would incur the expense of establishing a substantial trade or business in the other State simply to obtain the benefits of the Convention. A similar rationale underlies other tests in Article 22.

While these tests provide useful surrogates for identifying actual intent, these mechanical tests cannot account for every case in which the taxpayer was not treaty shopping. Accordingly, Article 22 also includes a provision (paragraph 6) authorizing the competent authority of a Contracting State to grant benefits that would not otherwise be granted. While an analysis under paragraph 6 may well differ from that under one of the other tests of Article 22, its objective is the same: to identify investors whose residence in the other State can be explained by factors other than a purpose to derive treaty benefits.

Article 22 and the anti-abuse provisions of domestic law complement each other, as Article 22 effectively determines whether an entity has a sufficient nexus to the Contracting State to be treated as a resident for treaty purposes, while domestic anti-abuse provisions (e.g., business purpose, substance-over-form, step transaction or conduit principles) determine whether a particular transaction should be recast in accordance with its substance. If the entity is determined to be the beneficial owner of the income after application of these internal law principles, Article 22 then will be applied to the beneficial owner to determine if that person is entitled to the benefits of the Convention with respect to such income.

Structure of the Article

The structure of the Article is as follows: Paragraph 1 states the general rule that residents are entitled to benefits only to the extent that the resident is described in a series of attributes of a resident of a Contracting State, the presence of any one of which will entitle that person to benefits of the Convention. Paragraph 2 provides that benefits are available to certain entities that are not-for-profit organizations. Paragraph 3 provides for limited so-called "derivative benefits" with respect to dividends, interest, and royalties to a company resident in the other Contracting State. Paragraph 4 limits treaty benefits in certain "triangular" cases. Paragraph 5 provides that the competent authorities may consult in order to develop commonly agreed understandings and applications of the provisions of the Article. Paragraph 6 provides that benefits also may be granted if the competent authority of the State from which benefits are claimed determines that it is appropriate to provide benefits in that case. Paragraph 7 defines terms used in this Article.

Paragraph 1

Paragraph 1 provides that a resident of a Contracting State (as determined under Article 4 (Resident)) will be entitled to some or all of the benefits otherwise accorded to residents of a Contracting State under the Convention only to the extent that the resident is described in one of the subparagraphs of paragraph 1. The benefits otherwise accorded to residents under the Convention include all limitations on source-based taxation under Articles 6 through 21, the treaty-based relief from double taxation provided by Article 23 (Relief from Double Taxation), and the protection afforded to residents of a Contracting State under Article 24(Non-Discrimination). Some provisions do not require that a person be a resident in order to enjoy the benefit of those provisions. These include paragraph 1 of Article 24 (Non-Discrimination), Article 25 (Mutual Agreement Procedure), and Article 27 (Diplomatic Agents and Consular Officers). Article 22 accordingly does not limit the availability of the benefits of these provisions.

Paragraph 1 has seven subparagraphs, each of which describes a category of residents that are entitled to some or all of the benefits of the Convention. It is intended that the provisions of paragraph 1 will be self-executing. Unlike the provisions of paragraph 6, discussed below, claiming benefits under paragraph 1 does not require advance competent authority ruling or approval. The tax authorities may, of course, on review, determine that the taxpayer has improperly interpreted the paragraph and is not entitled to the benefits claimed.

Individuals -- Subparagraph 1(a)

Subparagraph (a) provides that individual residents of a Contracting State will be entitled to all treaty benefits. If such an individual receives income as a nominee on behalf of a third country resident, benefits may be denied under the respective articles of the Convention by the requirement that the beneficial owner of the income be a resident of a Contracting State.

United States citizens or green card holders that are not resident in Switzerland come within the scope of subparagraph (a) if they would be considered residents of the United States under Article 4. See subparagraph 1(a) of Article 4.

Governmental Entities -- Subparagraph 1(b)

Subparagraph (b) provides that certain governmental entities will be entitled to all benefits of the Convention. The relevant persons are the Contracting States, political subdivisions or local authorities thereof, or agencies or instrumentalities of such a State, subdivision, or authority. This includes state, cantonal and local governments in addition to the federal government but does not include all entities described in subparagraph 1(b) of Article 4 (Resident). For example, this definition does not include pension trusts or funds that provide pension benefits to employees or former employees of a Contracting State, although such pension trusts may qualify under paragraph 2.

Active trade or business test - Subparagraph 1(c)

Subparagraph 1(c) sets forth a test under which a resident of a Contracting State that is not generally entitled to benefits of the Convention under the other subparagraphs of paragraph 1 may receive treaty benefits with respect to certain items of income that are connected to an active trade or business conducted in its State of residence.

Subparagraph 1(c) sets forth a three-pronged test that must be satisfied in order for a resident of a Contracting State to be entitled to the benefits of the Convention with respect to a particular item of income. First, the resident must be engaged in the active conduct or a trade or business in its State of residence. Second, the income derived from the other State must be derived in connection with, or be incidental to, that trade or business. Third, the Protocol provides that the trade or business must be substantial in relation to the activity in the other State that generated the income, if the income arises from a transaction with a related party. These determinations are made separately for each item of income derived from the other Contracting State. It therefore is possible that a person would be entitled to the benefits of the Convention with respect to one item of income but not with respect to another. For instance, dividends received from a subsidiary in the other State might be entitled to the benefits of the Convention, but other dividends might not be so entitled. If a resident of a Contracting State is entitled to treaty benefits with respect to a particular item of income under subparagraph 1(c), the resident is entitled to all benefits of the Convention insofar as they affect the taxation of that item of income in the other State. Set forth below is a discussion of each of the three prongs of the test under paragraph 1(c). Paragraph 4 of the Memorandum of Understanding provides further clarification of the test and examples of how the test is applied in practice.

Trade or Business

Paragraph 7(a) of the Protocol provides a definition of "trade or business" that is modeled on the regulations issued under section 367(a) of the Code. Whether the activities of a foreign corporation constitute an active trade or business is determined under all of the facts and circumstances. It further provides that a trade or business comprises activities that constitute (or could constitute) an independent economic enterprise carried on for profit. The active conduct of a trade or business need not involve manufacturing or sales activities but may instead involve services. The activities conducted by the resident ordinarily must include every operation which forms a part of, or a step in, a process by which an enterprise may earn income or profit in order to constitute a trade or business. The Protocol provides that a resident of a Contracting State actively conducts a trade or business if it regularly performs active and substantial management and operational functions through its own officers or staff of employees. One or more of such activities may be carried out by independent contractors under the direct control of the resident. However, in determining whether the corporation actively conducts a trade or business, the activities of independent contractors are disregarded.

An item of income will be considered to be earned in connection with, or to be incidental to, an active trade or business in a Contracting State if the resident claiming the benefits is itself engaged in business, or it is deemed to be so engaged through the activities of related persons that are residents of one of the Contracting States. Thus, for example, a resident of a Contracting State could claim benefits with respect to an item of income earned by an operating subsidiary in the other Contracting State but derived by the resident indirectly through a wholly-owned holding company resident in the other Contracting State and interposed between it and the operating subsidiary.

Notwithstanding this general definition of trade or business, subparagraph 1(c) provides that the business of making, managing or simply holding investments, when part of banking, insurance or securities activities conducted by a bank, insurance company, or registered securities dealer, will be considered to be a trade or business. Conversely, such activities conducted by a person other than a bank, insurance company or registered securities dealer will not be considered to be the conduct of an active trade or business, nor would they be considered to be the conduct of an active trade or business if conducted by a bank, insurance company or registered securities dealer but not in the ordinary course of business. This rule does not affect the status of investment advisors or others who are actively conducting the business of managing investments that are beneficially owned by others.

Because a headquarters operation is in the business of managing investments, a company whose sole functions are headquarters functions (including group financing) will not be considered to be engaged in an active trade or business for purposes of subparagraph 1(c), although if it satisfies specified standards it may be entitled to benefits under subparagraph 1(d).

Derived in Connection With Requirement

Paragraph 4 of the Memorandum of Understanding provides that income is derived in connection with a trade or business if the income-producing activity in the other Contracting State is a line of business that forms a part of, or is complementary to, the trade or business conducted in the State of residence of the income recipient. Although no definition of the terms "forms a part of" or "complementary" is set forth in the Convention, it is intended that a business activity generally will be considered to "form a part of" a business activity conducted in the other Contracting State if the two activities involve the design, manufacture or sale of the same products or type of products, or the provision of similar services. In order for two activities to be considered to be "complementary," the activities need not relate to the same types of products or services, but they should be part of the same overall industry and be related in the sense that the success or failure of one activity will tend to result in success or failure of the other. In cases in which more than one trade or business is conducted in the other Contracting State and only one of the trades or businesses forms a part of or is complementary to a trade or business conducted in the State of residence, it is necessary to identify the trade or business to which an item of income is attributable. Royalties generally will be considered to be derived in connection with the trade or business to which the underlying intangible property is attributable. Dividends will be deemed to be derived first out of earnings and profits of the treaty-benefitted trade or business, and then out of other earnings and profits. Interest income may be allocated under any reasonable method consistently applied. A method that conforms to U.S. principles for expense allocation will be considered a reasonable method. The Memorandum of Understanding includes examples illustrating the application of these rules.

Finally, a resident in one of the States also will be entitled to the benefits of the Convention with respect to income derived from the other State if the income is "incidental" to the trade or business conducted in the recipient's State of residence. The Memorandum of Understanding specifies that income derived from a State will be incidental to a trade or business conducted in the other State if the production of such income facilitates the conduct of the trade or business in the other State. An example of incidental income is interest income earned from the short-term investment of working capital of a resident of a Contracting State in securities issued by persons in the other Contracting State.

Substantiality

As indicated above, paragraph 7(b) of the Protocol provides that income that a resident of a Contracting State derives from a related party will be entitled to the benefits of the Convention under subparagraph 1(c) only if the income is derived in connection with a trade or business conducted in the recipient's State of residence and that trade or business is "substantial" in relation to the income-producing activity in the other State. A recipient is related to the payor of the income if the recipient owns, directly or indirectly, 10 percent or more of the shares or other comparable rights in the payor.

Paragraph 7(b) of the Protocol provides that whether a trade or business of the income recipient is "substantial" in relation to the activity carried on in the other Contracting State will be determined based on all the facts and circumstances. The determination takes into account the comparative sizes of the trades or businesses in each Contracting State (measured by reference to asset values, income and payroll expenses), the nature of the activities performed in each Contracting State, and, in cases where a trade or business is conducted in both Contracting States, the relative contributions made to that trade or business in each Contracting State. In making each determination or comparison, due regard is given to the relative sizes of the U.S. and Swiss economies.

Headquarters company test

Paragraph 1(d) provides that a resident of one of the Contracting States is entitled to all the benefits of the Convention if that person functions as a recognized headquarters company for a multinational corporate group. All corporations that the headquarters company supervises are included in the group, but the companies being supervised need not include the entire multinational group, but may be part of a larger group of companies. The headquarters company does not have to own shares in the companies that it supervises. In order to be considered a headquarters company, the person must meet several requirements that are enumerated in paragraph 7(b). These requirements are discussed below.

Overall Supervision and Administration

Subparagraph 7(b)(i) provides that the person must provide a substantial portion of the overall supervision and administration of the group. This activity may include group financing, but group financing may not be the principal activity of the person functioning as the headquarters company. A person only will be considered to engage in supervision and administration if it engages in a number of the following activities: group financing, pricing, marketing, internal auditing, internal communications, and management. Other activities also could be part of the function of supervision and administration.

In determining whether a "substantial portion" of the overall supervision and administration of the group is provided by the headquarters company, its headquarter-related activities must be substantial in relation to the same activities for the same group performed by other entities.

Subparagraph 7(b)(i) does not require that the group that is supervised include persons in the other State. However, it is anticipated that in most cases the group will include such persons, due to the requirement discussed below that the income derived by the headquarters company be derived in connection with or be incidental to an active trade or business supervised by the headquarter company.

Active Trade or Business

Subparagraph 7(b)(ii) is the first of several requirements intended to ensure that the relevant group is truly "multinational." This subparagraph provides that the corporate group supervised by the headquarters company must consist of corporations resident in, and engaged in active trades or businesses in, at least five countries. Furthermore, at least five countries must contribute substantially to the income generated by the group, as the rule requires that the business activities carried on in each of the five countries (or five groupings of countries) generate at least 10 percent of the gross income of the group. For purposes of the 10 percent gross income requirement, the income from multiple countries may be aggregated, as long as there are at least five individual countries or groupings that each satisfy the 10 percent requirement. If the gross income requirement under this subparagraph is not met for a taxable year, the taxpayer may satisfy this requirement by averaging the ratios for the four years preceding the taxable year.

Single Country Limitation

Subparagraph 7(b)(iii) provides that the business activities carried on in any one country other than the headquarters company's state of residence must generate less than 50 percent of the gross income of the group. If the gross income requirement under this subparagraph is not met for a taxable year, the taxpayer may satisfy this requirement by averaging the ratios for the four years preceding the taxable year.

Other State Gross Income Limitation

Subparagraph 7(b)(iv) provides that no more than 25 percent of the headquarters company's gross income may be derived from the other State. Thus, if the headquarter company's gross income for the taxable year is $200, no more than $50 of this amount may be derived from the other State. If the gross income requirement under this subparagraph is not met for a taxable year, the taxpayer may satisfy this requirement by averaging the ratios for the four years preceding the taxable year.

Independent Discretionary Authority

Subparagraph 7(b)(v) requires that the headquarters company have and exercise independent discretionary authority to carry out the functions referred to in clause (i). Thus, if the headquarters company was nominally responsible for group financing, pricing, marketing and other management functions, but merely implemented instructions received from another entity, the headquarters company would not be considered to have and exercise independent discretionary authority with respect to these functions. This determination is made individually for each function. For instance, a headquarters company could be nominally responsible for group financing, pricing, marketing and internal auditing functions, but another entity could be actually directing the headquarters company as to the group financing function. In such a case, the headquarters company would not be deemed to have independent discretionary authority for group financing, but it might have such authority for the other functions. Functions for which the headquarters company does not have and exercise independent discretionary authority are considered to be conducted by an entity other than the headquarters company for purposes of clause (i).

Income Taxation Rules

Subparagraph 7(b)(vi) requires that the headquarters company be subject to the generally applicable income taxation rules in its country of residence. This reference should be understood to mean that the company must be subject to the income taxation rules to which a company engaged in the active conduct of a trade or business would be subject. Thus, if one of the Contracting States introduced special taxation legislation that would impose a lower rate of income tax on headquarters companies than was imposed on companies engaged in the active conduct of a trade or business, or would provide for an artificially low taxable base for such companies, a headquarters company subject to these rules would not be entitled to the benefits of the Convention under subparagraph 1(d).

In Connection With or Incidental to Trade or Business

Finally, subparagraph 7(b)(vii) requires that the income derived in the other Contracting State be derived in connection with or be incidental to the active business activities referred to in clause (ii). This determination is made under the principles set forth in subparagraph 1(c). For instance, if a Swiss company that satisfied the other requirements in subparagraph 7(b) acted as a headquarters company for a group that included a United States corporation, the group was engaged in the design and manufacture of computer software, but the U.S. company was also engaged in the design and manufacture of photocopying machines, the income that the Swiss company derived from the United States would have to be derived in connection with or be incidental to the income generated by the computer business in order to be entitled to the benefits of the Convention under subparagraph 1(d). Similarly, interest income received from the U.S. company also would be entitled to the benefits of the Convention under this paragraph as long as the interest was attributable to a trade or business supervised by the headquarters company. Interest income derived from an unrelated party would normally not, however, satisfy the requirements of this subparagraph.

Publicly traded entities

Subparagraph 1(e) applies to two categories of corporations: publicly-traded corporations and subsidiaries of publicly-traded corporations. Clause (i) provides that a company will be entitled to all the benefits of the Convention if the principal class of shares of the company is primarily and regularly traded on a recognized stock exchange.

The term "recognized stock exchange" is defined in subparagraph 7(a). Subparagraph 7(a) provides that the term "recognized stock exchange" means (i) any Swiss stock exchange on which registered dealings take place; (ii) the NASDAQ System and any stock exchange registered as a national securities exchange with the Securities and Exchange Commission; (iii) the stock exchanges of Amsterdam, Frankfurt, London, Milan, Madrid, Paris, Tokyo and Vienna; and (iv) any other stock exchange agreed upon by the competent authorities of both Contracting States.

The term "principal class of shares" is not defined in the Convention, but will be interpreted by the United States, consistently with other recent U.S. tax treaties and the U.S. Model, to mean that class of shares that represents the majority of the voting power and value of the company. In most cases, this class will be the ordinary or common shares of the company. If the company has more than one class of shares, it is necessary as an initial matter to determine whether one of the classes accounts for more than half of the voting power and value of the company. If so, then only those shares are considered for purposes of the regular trading requirement. If no single class of shares accounts for more than half of the company's voting power and value, it is necessary to identify a group of two or more classes of the company's voting power and value, and then to determine whether each class of shares in this group satisfy the regular trading requirement. Although in a particular case involving a company with several classes of shares it is conceivable that more than one group of classes could be identified that account for more than 50% of the shares, it is only necessary for one such group to satisfy the requirements of this subparagraph in order for the company to be entitled to benefits. Benefits would not be denied to the company even if a second, non-qualifying, group of shares with more than half of the company's voting power and value could be identified.

The term "regularly traded" is not defined in the Convention. In accordance with paragraph 2 of Article 3 (General Definitions), this term will be defined by reference to the domestic tax laws of the Contracting State from which treaty benefits are sought (i.e., the source State). In the case of the United States, this term is understood to have the meaning it has under Treas. Reg. section 1.884-5(d)(4)(i)(B), relating to the branch tax provisions of the Code. Under these regulations, a class of shares is considered to be "regularly traded" if two requirements are met: trades in the class of shares are made in more than de minimis quantities on at least 60 days during the taxable year, and the aggregate number of shares in the class traded during the year is at least 10 percent of the average number of shares outstanding during the year. Sections 1.884-5(d)(4)(i)(A), (ii) and (iii) will not be taken into account for purposes of defining the term "regularly traded" under the Convention.

The regular trading requirement can be met by trading on any recognized exchange or exchanges located in either Contracting State. Trading on one or more recognized stock exchanges may be aggregated for purposes of this requirement. Thus, a U.S. company could satisfy the regularly traded requirement through trading, in whole or in part, on a recognized stock exchange located in Switzerland or certain third countries. Authorized but unissued shares are not considered for purposes of this test.

Subsidiaries of Publicly-Traded Corporations

Clause (ii) of subparagraph 1(e) provides a test under which certain companies that are controlled by one or more companies, each of which is a resident of one of the Contracting States that is entitled to the benefits of the Convention by reason of the publicly-traded test of subparagraph 1(e)(i), may be entitled to the benefits of the Convention. Under this test, a company will qualify for benefits if one or more companies described in paragraph 1(e)(i) are the ultimate beneficial owners of a predominant interest in the company. The predominant interest test will be interpreted consistently with the predominant interest test that applies for purposes of subparagraph 1(f) and which generally requires a direct, or indirect, interest of more than 50 percent. Thus, for example, a Swiss resident corporation, all the shares in which are owned by another Swiss resident corporation, will qualify for benefits under the Convention if the principal class of shares of the Swiss parent are primarily and regularly traded on the Frankfurt stock exchange unless one or more persons who do not qualify for benefits under the Convention are the beneficial owners of other types of interests in the subsidiary that constitute a predominant interest under the principles of subparagraph 1(f). However, the Swiss company would not qualify for benefits under subparagraph 1(e)(ii) if the publicly-traded parent company were a resident of Germany, not of the United States or Switzerland. The requirement that the company described in clause 1(e)(ii) be a subsidiary of a resident of one of the Contracting States is confirmed in paragraph 5 of the Memorandum of Understanding.

This test differs from that under subparagraph 1(e)(i) in that 50 percent of the aggregate interests, not merely the class or classes accounting for more than 50 percent of the company's votes and value, must be held by publicly-traded companies described in subparagraph 1(e)(i). Thus, the test under subparagraph 1(e)(ii) considers the ownership of every class of shares outstanding, as well as debt and contractual interests, while the test under subparagraph 1(e)(i) only considers those classes that account for a majority of the company's voting power and value.

Predominant interest test

Paragraph 1(f), as amplified by paragraph 8 of the Protocol, provides that certain legal entities may qualify for all the benefits of the Convention if they satisfy a "predominant interest" test. The test is also relevant for purposes of subparagraph (1)(e)(ii).

The predominant interest test performs the same function in the Convention as the so-called ownership/base erosion test found in recent U.S. tax treaties and the U.S. Model in that it looks to whether those that benefit from the Convention, whether through equity ownership or by receiving payments that erode the recipient's tax base, are qualified residents of one of the Contracting States. The predominant interest test was used in this context in order to blend certain principles found in Swiss domestic law with U.S. ownership/base erosion concepts.

The predominant interest test applies to a company, trust or estate that is a resident of a Contracting State. In order to be entitled to benefits under this paragraph, the entity must qualify under a two part test. Under the test, the benefits will be granted by one Contracting State to an entity resident in the other Contracting State, unless (1) persons not entitled to benefits under paragraphs 1(a),(b),(d),(e) or (g) are, in the aggregate, the ultimate beneficial owners of a predominant equity interest in the entity ("the ownership test"), and/or (2) such persons are, in the aggregate, the ultimate beneficial owners of a predominant interest, whether equity, debt or contractual, in the entity ("the combined test"). A predominant interest is a direct, or indirect, interest of more than 50 percent.

In order to determine whether these requirements have been met, it is first determined under the ownership test whether a predominant interest in the equity interests in the entity is ultimately owned, in the aggregate, by persons not entitled to benefits under the treaty. For example, if the shares of a Swiss company are owned by another Swiss company that is wholly owned by residents of a third country, that Swiss company would not pass the ownership test, because more than 50 percent of its shares, the predominant interest, is indirectly owned by the third-country residents not entitled to benefits under the treaty. Treaty benefits would not be extended to that Swiss company even if the company satisfied the combined test. If the ownership test has been met, then the combined test is applied.

Under the combined test, it is determined whether persons not entitled to benefits hold, in the aggregate, a predominant interest in the entity. In making the determination, the various equity, debt and contractual relationships of the company or a related party are considered. Under paragraph 8 of the Protocol, the parties agreed to consider, in making the determination, other contractual interests, in addition to the equity interest, that persons may have in the entity and the extent to which such persons receive, or have the right to receive, directly or indirectly, payments from that entity (including payments for interest or royalties, whether or not at arm's length) that reduce the amount of the entity's taxable income. In determining the amount of deductible payments, payments at arm's length for the purchase, use of, or right to use tangible property in the ordinary course of business or for services are disregarded, regardless of whether the recipient of the payments is a person entitled to benefits of the Convention under paragraph 2. Depreciation and amortization deductions, which are not "payments," are disregarded as well.

It is possible that no person would have a predominant interest in a company, estate or trust, in which case it would satisfy the requirements of subparagraph (f). Accordingly, a company whose shares and debt obligations are widely held by unrelated persons generally would satisfy the predominant interest test.

Paragraph 6 of the Memorandum of Understanding includes examples that illustrate the rules of this paragraph.

Family foundation test

Paragraph 1(g) provides that family foundations that are resident in Switzerland may qualify for all the benefits of the Convention except in certain circumstances. Family foundations are entities created under Swiss law by individuals to benefit certain beneficiaries. A family foundation will not qualify for benefits if the founder or the majority of the beneficiaries are persons not entitled to benefits under paragraph 1(a). A family foundation also would fail to qualify for benefits if 50 percent or more of the income of the foundation could benefit persons not entitled to benefits under paragraph 1(a). For this purpose, a family foundation may be disqualified even if all the income is in fact distributed to Swiss or U.S. persons, if there is no restriction that prevents the income from being distributed to persons who are not entitled to benefits. Thus, if the income of the foundation could be distributed on a discretionary basis to a number of persons and there were no restriction that prevented non-qualifying individuals from receiving the income, the family foundation would not qualify under this provision.

Paragraph 2

Paragraph 2 provides that pension trusts and not-for-profit organizations described in subparagraph 1(c) of Article 4 (Resident) will be entitled to all the benefits of the Convention, as long as more than half of the beneficiaries, members or participants of the organization are entitled to the benefits of the Convention. An organization referred to in this provision is generally exempt from tax in its State of residence and is either (i) an entity that provides pensions, retirement or employee benefits and that is established by a person resident in that State; or (ii) an entity that is organized and maintained in that State for religious, charitable, educational, scientific, cultural or other public purposes. For purposes of this provision, the term "beneficiaries" should be understood to refer to the persons receiving benefits from the organization.

Paragraph 3

Paragraph 3 sets forth a limited derivative benefits test. In general, a derivative benefits test entitles the resident of a State to treaty benefits if the beneficial owner of the resident would have been entitled to the same benefit had the income in question flowed directly to that owner. Paragraph 3 provides a derivative benefits test under which a company that is a resident of a Contracting State may be entitled to the benefits of Articles 10 (Dividends), 11 (Interest) and 12 (Royalties). In order to be entitled to the enumerated benefits of the Convention under this paragraph, the company must meet an ownership test, a base reduction test, and a derivative benefits test. Subparagraph 3(a) sets forth the ownership test and base reduction test. Subparagraph 3(b) sets forth the derivative benefits test.

Subparagraph 3(a)(i) provides that more than 30 percent of the vote and value of each class of the company's shares must be owned by residents of a Contracting State that are entitled to benefits under paragraph 1, other than under subparagraph 1(c). Ownership must be direct. There is no limit on the number of shareholders.

Subparagraph 3(a)(ii) provides that more than 70 percent of each class of shares must be owned directly by any number of residents of a Contracting State entitled to benefits under paragraph 1 or persons that are residents of member states of the European Union, European

Economic Area or North American Free Trade Agreement that are described in subparagraph 3(b).

Under subparagraph 3(b), shares held by shareholder residents of member states of the European Union, the European Economic Area or parties to the North American Free Trade Agreement will be counted toward the 70 percent test only if three requirements are met. First, the person must be entitled to the benefits of an income tax treaty between its state of residence and the Contracting State from which treaty benefits are claimed. Second, the person must be described in one of the subparagraphs of paragraph 1, applied as if the person were a resident of the Contracting State in which the company claiming benefits is resident. Finally, the person must be entitled, under the income tax treaty between its state of residence and the Contracting State from which treaty benefits are claimed, to a rate of tax equal to or less than the rate provided under this Convention with respect to the income derived from that Contracting State.

Subparagraph 3(a)(iii) provides that the amount of expenses paid or payable by the company in question to persons not qualifying under subparagraphs 1(a), (b), (d), (e), (f) or (g) that are deductible from gross income must be less than 50 percent of the gross income of the company for that period. This test is applied for the fiscal period immediately preceding the period for which the qualifying person test is being applied. If it is the first fiscal period of the person, the test is applied for the current period.

The term "gross income" is not defined in the Convention. Thus, in accordance with paragraph 2 of Article 3 (General Definitions), in determining whether a person deriving income from U.S. sources is entitled to the benefits of the Convention pursuant to paragraph 3, the United States will ascribe to the term the meaning that it has in the United States. In such cases, "gross income" will be defined as gross receipts less cost of goods sold.

Paragraph 4

Paragraph 4 addresses the so-called "triangular case," in which a resident of Switzerland derives income from the United States through a permanent establishment in a third country that imposes little or no income tax liability on that income, and the income is not taxed by Switzerland under its system of taxing business profits. The Contracting States agreed that it would be inappropriate to grant full treaty benefits with respect to income derived in such a case. Therefore, paragraph 4 denies full treaty benefits with respect to the income if the combined tax on the income in Switzerland and the third country is less than 60 percent of the tax that would have been payable in Switzerland if the income were not attributable to the permanent establishment in the third country. Paragraph 4 further provides that any dividends, interest, or royalties derived in such a case shall be subject to a tax at source under domestic law, but at a rate not exceeding 15 percent of the gross amount. The paragraph is drafted reciprocally, but has no application with respect to benefits derived by a U.S. person, because the United States does not exempt the profits of a U.S. company attributable to its foreign permanent establishment.

In the case of a Swiss resident with a permanent establishment in a third country, the provisions of paragraph 4 do not apply to royalties received as compensation for the use of, or the right to use, intangible property produced or developed by the permanent establishment itself. The provisions of paragraph 4 also do not apply if the income derived from the other Contracting State is derived in connection with, or is incidental to, the active conduct of a trade or business by the permanent establishment in the third country. The business of making, managing or simply holding investments for the person's own account is not an active trade or business for this purpose unless the activities are banking, insurance or securities activities carried on by a bank, insurance company or registered securities dealer.

Paragraph 5

Paragraph 5 requires the competent authorities to consult in order to develop common applications and interpretations of the provisions of Article 22. As a result of such consultations they may publish guidance setting forth the terms of their agreements. Paragraph 5 also authorizes the competent authorities to exchange such information as is necessary to implement the provisions of Article 22. Such information exchange must be in accordance with the provisions of Article 26 (Exchange of Information).

Paragraph 6

Paragraph 6 provides that a resident of one of the Contracting States that is not otherwise entitled to the benefits of the Convention may be granted benefits under the Convention by the competent authority of the other Contracting State. This discretionary provision is included in recognition of the fact that, with the increasing scope and diversity of international economic relations, there may be cases where significant participation by third country residents in an enterprise of a Contracting State is warranted by sound business practice or long-standing business structures and does not necessarily indicate a motive of attempting to derive unintended Convention benefits.

The competent authority of a State will base a determination under this paragraph on whether the establishment, acquisition, or maintenance of the person seeking benefits under the Convention, or the conduct of such person's operations, has or had as one of its principal purposes the obtaining of benefits under the Convention. Thus, persons that establish operations in one of the States with a principal purpose of obtaining the benefits of the Convention ordinarily will not be granted relief under paragraph 6.

The competent authority may determine that the resident is entitled to all of the benefits of the Convention, or it may grant only certain benefits. For instance, it may grant benefits only with respect to a particular item of income in a manner similar to subparagraph 1(c). Further, the competent authority may set time limits on the duration of any relief granted.

It is assumed that, for purposes of implementing paragraph 6, a taxpayer will be permitted to present his case to the relevant competent authority for an advance determination based on the facts, and will not be required to wait until the tax authorities of one of the Contracting States have determined that benefits are denied. In these circumstances, it is also expected that if the competent authority determines that benefits are to be allowed, they will be allowed retroactively to the time of entry into force of the relevant treaty provision or the establishment of the structure in question, whichever is later. The competent authority of the source State will consult with the competent authority of the other State before making a determination.

Paragraph 7 of the Memorandum of Understanding sets forth the understanding of the negotiators that certain companies resident in one of the Contracting States are not engaged in treaty-shopping and thus will be entitled to all the benefits of the Convention. This determination is based on the fact that substantially all of the company is owned by companies that would be entitled to comparable benefits under a treaty with the United States and the entity's deductible payments also are made to entities that would be entitled to comparable benefits. Although a taxpayer may request an advance determination that it meets the requirements of paragraph 7 of the Memorandum of Understanding, it is not necessary.

The ownership test in paragraph 7 of the Memorandum of Understanding specifies that a company resident in a Contracting State shall be granted all the benefits of the Convention if seven or fewer residents that are residents of a member state of the European Union or of the European Economic Area or a party to the North American Free Trade Agreement that meet the requirements of subparagraph 3(b) of Article 22 are the ultimate beneficial owners of 95 percent or more of the aggregate vote and value of all of the company's shares. The ownership requirement is less than 100 percent to avoid denying benefits simply because there is a small non-qualified shareholder, while the limitation on the number of shareholders is set at seven in recognition of the fact that most of the companies that would want to use this provision will be subsidiaries of EU owners (i.e., in most cases there will be a single owner). The seven residents can be residents of different countries.

However, this ownership test will not be met, and benefits will not be granted, if the majority of a "disproportionate" class of shares is held by persons other than residents of a member state of the European Union or of the European Economic Area or a party to the North American Free Trade Agreement that meet the requirements of subparagraph 3(b) of Article 22. In general, a class of shares is "disproportionate" for these purposes if they entitle the shareholder to a disproportionately higher participation in the earnings that the company generates in the other State through particular assets or activities of the company. Such participation may take any form, including dividends or redemption payments. Such a class of shares would include so-called alphabet stock or tracking stock that entitles the holder to earnings produced by a particular division or subsidiary of the company in the source State. This provision applies if the disproportionate class of shares is issued by the company claiming benefits, or by a company that controls the company claiming benefits. In this context, control does not require majority ownership.

Paragraph 7 of the Memorandum of Understanding also includes a base erosion test that must be met in order for the competent authority to grant benefits under this provision. In order to satisfy this test, the amount of the company's expenses (including payments for interest or royalties, but not payments at arm's length for the purchase or use of or the right to use tangible property in the ordinary course of business or remuneration at arm's length for services) deductible from gross income that are paid or payable by the company for its preceding fiscal period to persons that are not residents of a member state of the European Union or of the European Economic Area or a party to the North American Free Trade Agreement that meet the requirements of subparagraph 3(b) of Article 22 must be less than 50 percent of the gross income of the company for that period.

Paragraph 7 of the Memorandum of Understanding cross-references subparagraph 3(b). Therefore, ownership by, or payments to, a resident of a member state of the European Union or of the European Economic Area or a party to the North American Free Trade Agreement will not count toward disqualification only if the resident meets three tests. First, the person must be entitled to the benefits of an income tax treaty between its state of residence and the Contracting State from which treaty benefits are claimed. Second, the person must be described in one of the subparagraphs of paragraph 1 of Article 22, applied as if the person were a resident of the Contracting State in which the company claiming benefits is resident. Finally, the person must be entitled, under the income tax treaty between its state of residence and the Contracting State from which treaty benefits are claimed, to a rate of tax equal to or less than the rate provided under this Convention with respect to the income derived from that Contracting State.

Paragraph 7

Paragraph 7 defines key terms used in this Article, which are discussed above in connection with the relevant paragraphs.

Article 23 (Relief from Double Taxation)

This Article describes the manner in which each Contracting State undertakes to relieve double taxation. The United States uses the foreign tax credit method under its internal law, and by treaty. Switzerland uses a combination of credit, exemption and deduction methods, depending on the nature of the income involved.

Paragraph 1

Paragraph 1 sets forth rules for double taxation relief in Switzerland. Paragraph 1(a) deals with those items of income in respect of which double taxation is eliminated by Switzerland by means of exemption. Paragraph 1(b) deals with dividends, paragraph 1(c) deals with certain income on which the United States may impose tax at its full domestic tax, and paragraph 1(d) deals with U.S. social security benefits.

Paragraph 1(a) provides that a resident of Switzerland, deriving income subject to U.S. taxation under the Convention, will be exempt from Swiss taxation on such income subject to the provisions of paragraphs 1(b), (c) and (d), and 3. Thus, income, other than that specified in paragraphs 1(b), (c) and (d), and 3, is exempt from Swiss taxation if taxed in the United States under the provisions of the Convention. Gain from real property situated in the United States referred to in paragraph 2 of Article 13 (Gains) is only exempt from Swiss taxation if U.S. taxation on such gains is demonstrated by the Swiss resident. Switzerland may, in determining the tax on the remaining income of the resident, apply the rate of tax as if the exempted income had not been exempt (i.e., exemption with progression).

Paragraph 1(b) provides that, upon request and subject to the provisions of paragraph 1(c), Switzerland may grant tax relief to a Swiss resident on dividends that were taxed by the United States in accordance with the provisions of Article 10 (Dividends). The relief may consist of a credit against the Swiss tax equal to the U.S. tax on the dividend, a lump sum reduction of the Swiss tax, or a partial exemption from Swiss tax. The applicable relief and procedures are determined in accordance with Swiss internal law.

Paragraph 1(c) provides that Switzerland shall allow a deduction from income derived by a Swiss resident for the U.S. tax imposed on dividends under paragraph 2 of Article 10 (Dividends) and interest under paragraph 6 of Article 11 (Interest) that is not entitled to any reduction under those provisions. There is no reduction in the full U.S. tax rate under those provisions of the Convention for (1) a dividend from a Real Estate Investment Trust other than a dividend paid to an individual holding an interest less than ten percent in the Real Estate Investment Trust and (2) interest determined by reference to receipts, sales, income, profits, cash flow or certain other factors of the debtor or a related person to the extent not qualifying as portfolio interest and an excess inclusion with respect to a residual interest in a REMIC.

Paragraph 1(c) further provides that Switzerland shall allow a deduction from income derived by a Swiss resident for the U.S. tax imposed on income not qualifying for treaty benefits as a result of Article 22 (Limitation on Benefits). Thus, for example, a Swiss corporation that does not qualify for any treaty benefits would be taxed by Switzerland on the amount of a dividend from a U.S. corporation less the U.S. taxes withheld from the dividend.

Under paragraph 1(d), Swiss residents subject to U.S. taxation of social security benefits and other public pensions under paragraph 4 of Article 19 (Government Service and Social Security) will receive a deduction from Swiss taxable income of an amount equal to the tax levied in the United States on the benefits, plus an exemption of one-third of the net amount of such payment. Paragraph 4 of Article 19 provides that the United States will limit its taxation of social security and other public pensions paid to Swiss residents to 15 percent of the gross payment. See the Technical Explanation to paragraph 4 of Article 19 for an explanation of the manner in which double taxation is relieved as a result of these two provisions.

Paragraph 2

The United States agrees, in paragraph 2, to allow to its citizens and residents a credit against U.S. tax for income taxes paid to Switzerland. Paragraph 2 also provides that Switzerland's covered taxes are income taxes for U.S. foreign tax credit purposes. This provision is based on the Treasury Department's review of Switzerland's laws.

The credit under the Convention is allowed in accordance with the provisions and subject to the limitations of U.S. law, as that law may be amended over time, so long as the general principle of this Article (i.e., the allowance of a credit) is retained. Thus, although the Convention provides for a foreign tax credit, the terms of the credit are determined by the provisions, at the time a credit is given, of the U.S. statutory credit.

Paragraph 2 also provides for a deemed-paid credit, consistent with section 902 of the Code, to a U.S. corporation in respect of dividends received from a corporation resident in Switzerland of which the U.S. corporation owns at least 10 percent of the voting stock. This credit is for the tax paid by the Swiss corporation on the earnings out of which the dividends are considered paid.

As indicated, the U.S. credit under the Convention is subject to the various limitations of U.S. law (see Code sections 901 - 908). For example, the credit against U.S. tax generally is limited to the amount of U.S. tax due with respect to net foreign source income within the relevant foreign tax credit limitation category (see Code section 904(a) and (d)), and the dollar amount of the credit is determined in accordance with U.S. currency translation rules (see, e.g., Code section 986). Similarly, U.S. law applies to determine carryover periods for excess credits and other inter-year adjustments. When the alternative minimum tax is due, the alternative minimum tax foreign tax credit generally is limited in accordance with U.S. law to 90 percent of alternative minimum tax liability. Furthermore, nothing in the Convention prevents the limitation of the U.S. credit from being applied on a per-country basis, an overall basis, or to particular categories of income (see, e.g., Code section 865(h)).

Paragraph 3

Paragraph 3 provides special rules for the tax treatment in both States of certain types of income derived from U.S. sources by U.S. citizens who are resident in Switzerland. Since U.S. citizens are subject to United States tax at ordinary progressive rates on their worldwide income, regardless of residence, the U.S. tax on the U.S. source income of a U.S. citizen resident in Switzerland may exceed the U.S. tax that may be imposed under the Convention on an item of U.S. source income derived by a resident of Switzerland who is not a U.S. citizen.

Subparagraph (a) of paragraph 3 provides special rules for Switzerland that will apply with respect to items of income that would be either exempt from U.S. tax or subject to reduced rates of U.S. tax under the provisions of the Convention when received by residents of Switzerland who are not U.S. citizens. Switzerland will apply the relief provisions of paragraph 1 to U.S.

citizens resident in Switzerland as if the amount of U.S. taxes paid in respect of such profits, income or gains were the amount of U.S. taxes paid by a Swiss resident not a U.S. citizen. Thus, if a U.S. citizen resident in Switzerland receives U.S. source portfolio dividends, the foreign tax credit granted by Switzerland under paragraph 1(b)(i) would be limited to 15 percent of the dividend -- the U.S. tax that may be imposed under subparagraph (2) of Article 10 (Dividends) -- even if the shareholder is subject to U.S. net income tax because of his U.S. citizenship. With respect to royalty or interest income, Switzerland would not be required to provide any relief to the extent that its residents are exempt from U.S. tax on these classes of income under the provisions of Articles 11 (Interest) and 12 (Royalties).

Paragraph 3(b) eliminates the potential for double taxation that can arise because subparagraph 3(a) provides that Switzerland need not provide full relief for the U.S. tax imposed on its citizens resident in Switzerland. The subparagraph provides that the United States will credit the income tax paid or accrued to Switzerland, after the application of subparagraph 3(a). It further provides that in allowing the credit, the United States will not reduce its tax below the amount that is taken into account in Switzerland in applying subparagraph 3(a). Since the income described in paragraph 3 is U.S. source income, special rules are required to resource some of the income to Switzerland in order for the United States to be able to credit the Swiss tax. This resourcing is provided for in subparagraph 3(c), which deems the items of income referred to in subparagraph 3(a) to be from Swiss sources to the extent necessary to avoid double taxation under paragraph 3(b). The rules of paragraph 3(c) apply only for purposes of determining U.S. foreign tax credits with respect to taxes referred to in paragraphs 2(a) and 3 of Article 2 (Taxes Covered).

The following two examples illustrate the application of paragraph 3 in the case of a U.S. source portfolio dividend received by a U.S. citizen resident in Switzerland. In both examples, the U.S. rate of tax on Swiss residents under paragraph 2(b) of Article 10 (Dividends) of the Convention is 15 percent. In both examples the U.S. income tax rate on the U.S. citizen is 36 percent. In example I, the combined Swiss income tax rate (federal and cantonal) on its resident (the U.S. citizen) is 25 percent (below the U.S. rate), and in example II, the Swiss rate on its resident is 40 percent (above the U.S. rate).

	Example I	Example II
Paragraph 3(a)		
U.S. dividend declared	$100.00	$100.00
Notional U.S. withholding tax per Article 10(2)(b)	15.00	15.00
Swiss taxable income	100.00	100.00
Swiss tax before credit	25.00	40.00
Swiss foreign tax credit	15.00	15.00
Net post-credit Swiss tax	10.00	25.00

	Example I	Example II
Paragraphs 3(b) and (c)		
U.S. pre-tax income	$100.00	$100.00
U.S. pre-credit citizenship tax	36.00	36.00
Notional U.S. withholding tax	15.00	15.00
U.S. tax available for credit	21.00	21.00
Income resourced from U.S. to Switzerland	27.77	58.33
U.S. tax on resourced income	10.00	21.00
U.S. credit for Swiss tax	10.00	21.00
Net post-credit U.S. tax	11.00	0.00
Total U.S. tax	26.00	15.00

In both examples, in the application of paragraph 3(a), Switzerland credits a 15 percent U.S. tax against its residence tax on the U.S. citizen. In example I the net Swiss tax after foreign tax credit is $10.00; in the second example it is $25.00. In the application of paragraphs 3(b) and (c), from the U.S. tax due before credit of $36.00, the United States subtracts the amount of the U.S. source tax of $15.00, against which no U.S. foreign tax credit is to be allowed. This provision assures that the United States will collect the tax that it is due under the Convention as the source country. In both examples, the maximum amount of U.S. tax against which credit for Swiss tax may be claimed is $21.00. Initially, all of the income in these examples was U.S. source. In order for a U.S. credit to be allowed for the full amount of the Swiss tax, an appropriate amount of the income must be resourced. The amount that must be resourced depends on the amount of Swiss tax for which the U.S. citizen is claiming a U.S. foreign tax credit. In example I, the Swiss tax was $10.00. In order for this amount to be creditable against U.S. tax, $27.77 ($10 divided by .36) must be resourced as Swiss source. When the Swiss tax is credited against the U.S. tax on the resourced Swiss income, there is a net U.S. tax of $11.00 due after credit. In example II, Swiss tax was $25 but, because the amount available for credit is reduced under subparagraph 3(c) by the amount of the U.S. source tax, only $21.00 is eligible for credit. Accordingly, the amount that must be resourced is limited to the amount necessary to ensure a foreign tax credit for $21 of Swiss tax, or $58.33 ($21 divided by .36). Thus, even though Swiss tax was $25.00 and the U.S. tax available for credit was $21.00, there is no excess credit available for carryover.

Relation to Other Articles

By virtue of the exception in paragraph 3(a) of Article 1 (Personal Scope), this Article is not subject to the saving clause of paragraph 2 of Article 1. Thus, the United States will allow a credit to its citizens and residents in accordance with the Article, even if a credit were not available under the Code.

The benefits of this Article are subject to the provisions of Article 22 (Limitation on Benefits). Thus, because Switzerland provides a foreign tax credit only by treaty, not domestic law, a Swiss resident would not be entitled to a foreign tax credit pursuant to this article unless it qualifies for treaty benefits under at least one of the tests of Article 22.

Article 24 (Non-discrimination)

This Article assures that nationals of a Contracting State, in the case of paragraph 1, and residents of a Contracting State, in the case of paragraphs 2 through 4, will not be subject, directly or indirectly, to discriminatory taxation in the other Contracting State. For this purpose, non-discrimination means providing national treatment. Not all differences in tax treatment, either as between nationals of the two States, or between residents of the two States, are violations of this national treatment standard. Rather, the national treatment obligation of this Article applies only if the nationals or residents of the two States are comparably situated.

Each of the relevant paragraphs of the Article provides that two persons that are comparably situated must be treated similarly. Although the actual words differ from paragraph to paragraph (e.g., paragraph 1 refers to two nationals "in the same circumstances," paragraph 2 refers to two enterprises "carrying on the same activities" and paragraph 4 refers to two enterprises that are "similar"), the common underlying premise is that if the difference in treatment is directly related to a tax-relevant difference in the situations of the domestic and foreign persons being compared, that difference is not to be treated as discriminatory (e.g., one person is taxable in a Contracting State on worldwide income and the other is not, or tax may be collectible from one person at a later stage, but not from the other). Other examples of such factors that can lead to non-discriminatory differences in treatment will be noted in the discussions of each paragraph.

The operative paragraphs of the Article also use different language to identify the kinds of differences in taxation treatment that will be considered discriminatory. For example, paragraphs 1 and 4 speak of "any taxation or any requirement connected therewith which is other or more burdensome," while paragraph 2 specifies that a tax "shall not be less favorably levied." Regardless of the difference in language, only differences in tax treatment that materially disadvantage the foreign person relative to the domestic person are properly the subject of the Article.

Paragraph 1

Paragraph 1 provides that a national of one Contracting State may not be subject to taxation or connected requirements in the other Contracting State that are other or more burdensome than the taxes and connected requirements imposed upon a national of that other State in the same circumstances. This language is consistent with the OECD Model.

As noted above, whether or not the two persons are both taxable on worldwide income is a significant circumstance for this purpose. The 1992 revision of the OECD Model added after the words "in the same circumstances", the phrase "in particular with respect to residence," reflecting the fact that under most countries' laws residents are taxable on worldwide income and nonresidents are not.

Because the relevant circumstances referred to relate, among other things, to taxation on worldwide income, paragraph 1 does not obligate the United States to apply the same taxing regime to a national of Switzerland who is not resident in the United States and a U.S. national who is not resident in the United States. United States citizens who are not residents of the United States but who are, nevertheless, subject to U.S. tax on their worldwide income are not in the same circumstances with respect to U.S. taxation as citizens of Switzerland who are not United States residents. To reflect the difference in the basis of taxation between the U.S. and other systems, the Convention states explicitly that U.S. citizens who are not residents of the United States but who are, nevertheless, subject to U.S. tax on their worldwide income, are not in the same circumstances with respect to U.S. taxation as nationals of Switzerland who are not U.S. residents. The underlying concept is essentially the same in the OECD Model and the Convention.

A national of a Contracting State is afforded protection under this paragraph even if the national is not a resident of either Contracting State. Thus, a U.S. citizen who is resident in a third country is entitled, under this paragraph, to the same treatment in Switzerland as a Swiss national who is in similar circumstances (i.e., presumably one who is resident in a third State). The term "national" in relation to a Contracting State is defined in paragraph 1(d) of Article 3 (General Definitions).

Like the prior Convention and the U.S. and OECD Models, the scope of paragraph 1 extends beyond individuals to cover juridical persons that are nationals of a Contracting State. The inclusion of juridical persons in paragraph 1, however, generally may add little as a practical matter to the scope of the Article as a whole. A corporation that is a national of Switzerland and is doing business in the United States is already protected, vis-a-vis a U.S. corporation, by paragraph 2. If a foreign corporation is not doing business in the United States it is, in relevant respect, in different circumstances from a U.S. corporation and is, therefore, not entitled to national treatment in the United States. With respect to U.S. nationals claiming non-discrimination protection from Switzerland, U.S. corporations that are "nationals" of the United States are also U.S. residents and are, therefore, protected by paragraphs 2 and 4 in any event.

Paragraph 2

Paragraph 2 of the Article, like the comparable paragraphs in the U.S. and OECD Models, provides that a Contracting State may not tax a permanent establishment of an enterprise of the other Contracting State less favorably than an enterprise of that first-mentioned State that is carrying on the same activities. This provision, however, does not obligate a Contracting State to grant to a resident of the other Contracting State any tax allowances, reliefs, etc., that it grants to its own residents on account of their civil status or family responsibilities. Thus, if an individual resident in Switzerland owns a Swiss enterprise that has a permanent establishment in the United States, in assessing income tax on the profits attributable to the permanent establishment, the United States is not obligated to allow to the Swiss resident the personal allowances for himself and his family that he would be permitted to take if the permanent establishment were a sole proprietorship owned and operated by a U.S. resident, even though the individual income tax rates would apply.

The fact that a U.S. permanent establishment of an enterprise of the other Contracting State is subject to U.S. tax only on income that is attributable to the permanent establishment, while a U.S. corporation engaged in the same activities is taxable on its worldwide income is not, in itself, a sufficient difference to deny national treatment to the permanent establishment. There are cases, however, where the two enterprises would not be similarly situated and differences in treatment may be warranted. For instance, it would not be a violation of the non-discrimination protection of paragraph 2 to require the foreign enterprise to provide information in a reasonable manner that may be different from the information requirements imposed on a resident enterprise, because information may not be as readily available to the Internal Revenue Service from a foreign as a domestic enterprise.

Section 1446 of the Code imposes on any partnership with income that is effectively connected with a U.S. trade or business the obligation to withhold tax on amounts allocable to a foreign partner. In the context of the Convention, this obligation applies with respect to a share of the partnership income of a Swiss resident partner that is attributable to a U.S. permanent establishment. There is no similar obligation with respect to the distributive shares of U.S. resident partners. It is understood, and confirmed in paragraph 9 of the Protocol, that this distinction is not a form of discrimination within the meaning of paragraph 2 of the Article. No distinction is made between U.S. and Swiss partnerships, since the law requires that partnerships of both U.S. and non-U.S. domicile withhold tax in respect of the partnership shares of non-U.S. partners. Furthermore, in distinguishing between U.S. and Swiss partners, the requirement to withhold on the Swiss but not the U.S. partner's share is not discriminatory taxation, but, like other withholding on nonresident aliens, is merely a reasonable method for the collection of tax from persons who are not continually present in the United States, and as to whom it otherwise may be difficult for the United States to enforce its tax jurisdiction. If tax has been over-withheld, the partner can, as in other cases of over-withholding, file for a refund. (The relationship between paragraph 2 and the imposition of the branch tax is dealt with below in the discussion of paragraph 6.)

Paragraph 3

Paragraph 3 prohibits discrimination in the allowance of deductions. When an enterprise of a Contracting State pays interest, royalties or other disbursements to a resident of the other Contracting State, the first-mentioned Contracting State must allow a deduction for those payments in computing the taxable profits of the enterprise under the same conditions as if the payment had been made to a resident of the first-mentioned Contracting State. An exception to this rule is provided for cases where the provisions of paragraph 1 of Article 9 (Associated Enterprises), paragraph 4 of Article 11 (Interest) or paragraph 4 of Article 12 (Royalties) apply, because all of these provisions permit the denial of deductions in certain circumstances in respect of transactions between related persons. This exception would include the denial or deferral of certain interest deductions under Code section 163(j).

The term "other disbursements" is understood to include a reasonable allocation of executive and general administrative expenses, research and development expenses and other expenses incurred for the benefit of a group of related persons which includes the person incurring the expense.

Paragraph 3 also provides that any debts of an enterprise of a Contracting State to a resident of the other Contracting State are deductible in the first-mentioned Contracting State for computing the capital tax of the enterprise under the same conditions as if the debt had been contracted to a resident of the first-mentioned State. Even though, for general purposes, the Convention covers only income taxes, under paragraph 5 of this Article, the non-discrimination provisions apply to all taxes levied in both Contracting States, at all levels of government. Thus, this provision is relevant for both Contracting States. Switzerland imposes capital taxes and in the United States such taxes are imposed by local governments.

Paragraph 4

Paragraph 4 requires that a Contracting State not impose other or more burdensome taxation or connected requirements on an enterprise of that State that is wholly or partly owned or controlled, directly or indirectly, by one or more residents of the other Contracting State, than the taxation or connected requirements that it imposes on other similar enterprises of that first-mentioned Contracting State. For this purpose it is understood that "similar" refers to similar activities or ownership of the enterprise.

The Tax Reform Act of 1986 ("TRA") introduced section 367(e)(2) of the Code which changed the rules for taxing corporations on certain distributions they make in liquidation. Prior to the TRA, corporations were not taxed on distributions of appreciated property in complete liquidation, although nonliquidating distributions of the same property, with several exceptions, resulted in corporate-level tax. In part to eliminate this disparity, the law now generally taxes corporations on the liquidating distribution of appreciated property. The Code provides an exception in the case of distributions by 80 percent or more controlled subsidiaries to their parent corporations, on the theory that the built-in gain in the asset will be recognized when the parent sells or distributes the asset. This exception does not apply to distributions to parent corporations that are tax-exempt organizations or, except to the extent provided in regulations, foreign corporations. The policy of the legislation is to collect one corporate-level tax on the liquidating distribution of appreciated property. If, and only if, that tax can be collected on a subsequent sale or distribution does the legislation defer the tax. Paragraph 8 of the Protocol confirms that the inapplicability of the exception to the tax on distributions to foreign parent corporations does not conflict with paragraph 4 of the Article. While a liquidating distribution to a U.S. parent will not be taxed, and, except to the extent provided in regulations, a liquidating distribution to a foreign parent will, paragraph 4 merely prohibits discrimination among corporate taxpayers on the basis of U.S. or foreign stock ownership. Eligibility for the exception to the tax on liquidating distributions for distributions to non-exempt, U.S. corporate parents is not based upon the nationality of the owners of the distributing corporation, but is based upon whether such owners would be subject to corporate tax if they subsequently sold or distributed the same property. Thus, the exception does not apply to distributions to persons that would not be so subject -- not only foreign corporations, but also tax-exempt organizations. A similar analysis applies to the treatment of section 355 distributions subject to section 367(e)(1).

For the reasons given above in connection with the discussion of paragraph 2 of the Article, Paragraph 8 of the Protocol provides that the provision in section 1446 of the Code for withholding of tax on non-U.S. partners does not violate paragraph 4 of the Article.

It is further understood that the ineligibility of a U.S. corporation with nonresident alien shareholders to make an election to be an "S" corporation does not violate paragraph 4 of the Article. If a corporation elects to be an S corporation (requiring 35 or fewer shareholders), it is generally not subject to income tax and the shareholders take into account their pro rata shares of the corporation's items of income, loss, deduction or credit. (The purpose of the provision is to allow an individual or small group of individuals to conduct business in corporate form while paying taxes at individual rates as if the business were conducted directly.) A nonresident alien does not pay U.S. tax on a net basis, and, thus, does not generally take into account items of loss, deduction or credit. Thus, the S corporation provisions do not exclude corporations with nonresident alien shareholders because such shareholders are foreign, but only because they are not net-basis taxpayers. Similarly, the provisions exclude corporations with other types of shareholders where the purpose of the provisions cannot be fulfilled or their mechanics implemented. For example, corporations with corporate shareholders are excluded because the purpose of the provisions to permit individuals to conduct a business in corporate form at individual tax rates would not be furthered by their inclusion.

Paragraph 5

As noted above, notwithstanding the specification of taxes covered by the Convention in Article 2 (Taxes Covered) for general purposes, for purposes of providing non-discrimination protection this Article applies to taxes of every kind and description imposed by a Contracting State or a political subdivision or local authority thereof. Customs duties are not considered to be taxes for this purpose.

Paragraph 6

Paragraph 6 of the Article confirms that no provision of the Article will prevent the United States from imposing the branch tax described in paragraph 7 of Article 10 (Dividends). Since imposition of the branch tax under the Convention is specifically sanctioned by paragraph 7 of Article 10 (Dividends), its imposition could not be precluded by Article 24, even without paragraph 5. Under the generally accepted rule of construction that the specific takes precedence over the general, the specific branch tax provision of Article 10 would take precedence over the more general national treatment provision of Article 24.

Relation to Other Articles

The saving clause of paragraph 2 of Article 1 (Personal Scope) does not apply to this Article, by virtue of the exceptions in paragraph 3(a) of Article 1. Thus, for example, a U.S. citizen who is a resident of Switzerland may claim benefits in the United States under this Article.

Nationals of a Contracting State may claim the benefits of paragraph 1 regardless of whether they are entitled to benefits under Article 22 (Limitation on Benefits). They may not claim the benefits of the other paragraphs of this Article with respect to an item of income unless they are generally entitled to treaty benefits with respect to that income under a provision of Article 22.

Article 25 (Mutual Agreement Procedure)

This Article provides the mechanism for taxpayers to bring to the attention of competent authorities issues and problems that may arise under the Convention. It also provides a mechanism for cooperation between the competent authorities of the Contracting States to resolve disputes and clarify issues that may arise under the Convention and to resolve cases of double taxation not provided for in the Convention. The Article also provides for the possibility of the use of arbitration to resolve disputes that cannot be settled by the competent authorities. The competent authorities of the two States are identified in paragraph 1(f) of Article 3 (General Definitions).

Paragraph 1

Paragraph 1 provides that where a resident of a Contracting State considers that the actions of one or both Contracting States will result in taxation that is not in accordance with the Convention he may present his case to the competent authority of his State of residence or nationality.

Although the typical cases brought under this paragraph will involve economic double taxation arising from transfer pricing adjustments, the scope of this paragraph is not limited to such cases. For example, if the United States treats income derived by a company resident in Switzerland as attributable to a U.S. permanent establishment, and the Swiss resident believes that the income is not attributable to a permanent establishment, or that no permanent establishment exists, the resident may bring a complaint under paragraph 1 to the competent authority of Switzerland.

It is not necessary for a person bringing a complaint first to have exhausted the remedies provided under the national laws of the Contracting States before presenting a case to the competent authorities, nor does the fact that the statute of limitations may have passed for seeking a refund preclude bringing a case to the competent authority. Although the Convention, like the U.S. Model, does not provide an explicit time limit within which a case must be brought, as a practical matter, taxpayers that wait too long to bring a case may be precluded from receiving relief as a result of the application of domestic statute of limitation rules. Under recent revisions to the Swiss law on limitation periods, formal request for competent authority relief, not mere notification that there is a problem, must be made within the 10 year period after the final assessment of Swiss taxes. If a request for relief is made after the expiration of the 10 year period, competent authority relief cannot be given by Switzerland. Because Switzerland cannot extend its period beyond the 10 years, the United States will use a reciprocal 10 year period under this article for accepting requests.

Paragraph 2

Paragraph 2 instructs the competent authorities in dealing with cases brought by taxpayers under paragraph 1. It provides that if the competent authority of the Contracting State to which the case is presented judges the case to have merit, and cannot reach a unilateral solution, it shall seek agreement with the competent authority of the other State such that taxation not in accordance with the Convention will be avoided.

The Convention does not include the language that is in the U.S. and OECD Models which requires the competent authorities to implement any agreement even if such implementation otherwise would be barred by the statute of limitations or by some other procedural limitation, such as a closing agreement. As noted above, Switzerland will apply a ten year notification period under the Convention for Swiss federal and cantonal taxation. Swiss competent authority relief may be given after the expiration of the 10 year period where the request for relief was received by Switzerland within the 10 year period. Reciprocally, the United States will implement a competent authority agreement only if the request is received within the 10-year period described above.

Paragraph 3

Paragraph 3 authorizes the competent authorities to resolve difficulties or doubts that may arise as to the application or interpretation of the Convention. The paragraph includes a non-exhaustive list of examples of the kinds of matters about which the competent authorities may reach agreement. This list is purely illustrative; it does not grant any authority that is not implicitly present as a result of the introductory sentence of paragraph 3. The competent authorities may, for example, agree to the same attribution of income, deductions, credits or allowances between an enterprise in one Contracting State and its permanent establishment in the other (subparagraph (a)) or between associated persons(subparagraph (b)). These allocations are to be made in accordance with the arm's length principle underlying Article 7 (Business Profits) and Article 9 (Associated Enterprises). Agreements reached under these subparagraphs may include agreement on a methodology for determining an appropriate transfer price, common treatment of a taxpayer's cost sharing arrangement, or upon an acceptable range of results under that methodology.

As indicated in subparagraphs (c), (d), (e) and (f), the competent authorities also may agree to settle a variety of conflicting applications of the Convention. They may agree to characterize particular items of income in the same way (subparagraph (c)), to characterize entities in a particular way (subparagraph (d)), to apply the same source rules to particular items of income (subparagraph (e)), and to adopt a common meaning of a term.

Subparagraph (g) makes clear that the competent authorities can agree to the common application, consistent with the objective of avoiding double taxation, of procedural provisions of the internal laws of the Contracting States, including those regarding penalties, fines and interest.

Finally, paragraph 3 authorizes the competent authorities to consult for the purpose of eliminating double taxation in cases not provided for in the Convention. This provision is intended to permit the competent authorities to implement the treaty in particular cases in a manner that is consistent with its expressed general purposes. It permits the competent authorities to deal with cases that are within the spirit of the provisions but that are not specifically covered. An example of such a case might be double taxation arising from a transfer pricing adjustment between two permanent establishments of a third-country resident, one in the United States and one in Switzerland. Since no resident of a Contracting State is involved in the case (both permanent establishments being residents of the third State), the Convention does not apply, but the competent authorities nevertheless may use the authority of the Convention to seek to prevent the double taxation.

Agreements reached by the competent authorities under paragraph 3 need not conform to the internal law provisions of either Contracting State. Paragraph 3 is not, however, intended to authorize the competent authorities to resolve problems of major policy significance that normally would be the subject of negotiations between the Contracting States themselves. For example, this provision would not authorize the competent authorities to agree to allow a U.S. foreign tax credit under the treaty for a tax imposed by Switzerland where that tax is not otherwise a covered tax and is not an identical or substantially similar tax imposed after the date of the signature of the Convention. In such a case, the creditability of the tax would be determined under the Code and regulations.

Paragraph 4

Paragraph 4 provides that the competent authorities may communicate with each other for the purpose of reaching an agreement. This makes clear that the competent authorities of the two Contracting States may communicate without going through diplomatic channels. Such communication may be in various forms, including, where appropriate, through face-to-face meetings of the competent authorities or their representatives.

Paragraph 5

Paragraph 5 provides that the competent authorities may prescribe procedures that are necessary to carry out the purposes of the Convention. These might include, for example, procedures relating to the verification of entitlement to treaty benefits under the provisions of Article 22 (Limitation on Benefits).

Paragraph 6

Paragraph 6 contains an arbitration procedure found in several recent U.S. tax treaties, although the arbitration procedures currently are operative only under the treaty with Germany. Paragraph 6 provides that where the competent authorities have been unable to resolve a disagreement regarding the application or interpretation of the Convention, the disagreement may, by mutual consent of the competent authorities and the affected taxpayers, be submitted for arbitration. Nothing in the provision requires that any case be submitted for arbitration. If a case is submitted to an arbitration board, however, the board's decision in that case will be binding on both Contracting States and the taxpayer(s) with respect to that case.

The arbitration procedures will not come into effect until the Contracting States have agreed through an exchange of diplomatic notes. It is anticipated that the two States will consider exchanging diplomatic notes implementing the arbitration procedure at such time the provisions under the other Conventions, and the European Communities agreement signed on 23 July, 1990, prove satisfactory to the competent authorities of both the United States and Switzerland. The arbitration procedures themselves also will be established through an exchange of notes.

Other Issues

Treaty effective dates and termination in relation to competent authority dispute resolution

A case may be raised by a taxpayer with respect to a year for which the Convention was in force after the Convention has been terminated. In such a case the ability of the competent authorities to act is limited. They may not exchange confidential information, nor may they reach a solution that varies from that under its law.

Triangular competent authority solutions

International tax cases may involve more than two taxing jurisdictions (e.g., transactions among a parent corporation resident in country A and its subsidiaries resident in countries B and C). As long as there is a complete network of treaties among the three countries, it should be possible under the full combination of bilateral authorities, for the competent authorities of the three States to work together on a three-sided solution. Although country A may not be able to give information received under Article 26 (Exchange of Information) from country B to the authorities of country C, if the competent authorities of the three countries are working together, it should not be a problem for them to arrange for the authorities of country B to give the necessary information directly to the tax authorities of country C, as well as to those of country A. Each bilateral part of the trilateral solution must, of course, not exceed the scope of the authority of the competent authorities under the relevant bilateral treaty.

Relation to Other Articles

This Article is not subject to the saving clause of paragraph 2 of Article 1 (Personal Scope) by virtue of the exceptions in paragraph 3(a) of that Article. Thus, rules, definitions, procedures, etc., that are agreed upon by the competent authorities under this Article may be applied by the United States with respect to its citizens and residents even if they differ from the comparable Code provisions. A person may seek relief under Article 25 regardless of whether he is generally entitled to benefits under Article 22 (Limitation on Benefits). As in all other cases, the competent authority is vested with the discretion to decide whether the claim for relief is justified.

Article 26 (Exchange of Information)

Paragraph 1

This Article provides for the exchange of information between the competent authorities of the Contracting States. The information to be exchanged is that which is necessary for carrying out the provisions of the Convention or for the prevention of tax fraud or the like in relation to the taxes covered by the Convention. The requirement that information be "necessary" to carry out these provisions, which also is contained in the OECD Model, consistently has been interpreted as requiring only that the information be "relevant" and it is not necessary for a requesting State to demonstrate that it would be disabled from enforcing its tax laws unless it obtained a particular item of information. Accordingly, the result should not be different under the Convention than under the U.S. Model, which refers to information that is "relevant" in order to remove any potential misimpression that the term "necessary" created a higher threshold than relevance.

The taxes covered by the Convention are those referred to in Article 2 (Taxes Covered). Although this provision is consistent with the OECD Model, it differs from the U.S. Model, which, for purposes of exchange of information, covers all taxes imposed by the two Contracting States. Many U.S. tax treaties differ from the U.S. Model in this respect, often due to the fact that the laws of the other treaty partner do not always permit exchange of information with respect to non-covered taxes. Switzerland was unable to extend the coverage beyond the taxes specified in Article 2.

Exchange of information in connection with the enforcement of domestic law is authorized insofar as the information is necessary to prevent tax fraud or the like. Under Paragraph 10 of the Protocol, tax fraud exists if the taxpayer has engaged in fraudulent conduct that causes or is intended to cause an illegal and substantial reduction in the amount of tax paid to a Contracting State. This definition generally is consistent with the domestic definitions of tax fraud in Switzerland and the United States.

The Protocol includes a non-exhaustive list of actions that will constitute tax fraud for purposes of the Convention. In general, these clarify for purposes of the Convention the Swiss concept of tax fraud, which exists if the taxpayer has falsified a document that the taxpayer uses or intends to use to justify the amount that the taxpayer has reported on its return. Examples of tax fraud cited in the Protocol include situations where a taxpayer uses, or has the intention to use, a forged or falsified document such as a double set of books, a false invoice, an incorrect balance sheet or profit and loss statement, or a fictitious order or, in general, a false piece of documentary evidence. Tax fraud also exists wherever a taxpayer wilfully files a falsified return for a corporation, partnership, or other associated entity, which causes an illegal substantial reduction in taxes due. The definition included in the Protocol also cites a concept ("Lugengebaude") where a taxpayer uses, or has the intention to use a "scheme of lies" to deceive the tax authorities.

The definition of tax fraud in the Protocol also includes acts that, at the time of the request, constitute fraudulent conduct with respect to which the requested Contracting State may obtain information under its laws or practices. Accordingly, if one of the Contracting States expands its concept of tax fraud, that State will be obligated to provide assistance to the other state on cases falling within that expanded definition of tax fraud.

The Protocol also contains a rule to deal with the situation where a taxpayer has falsified documents that the taxpayer is required to keep under the laws of the requesting Contracting State, but that are not required to be kept under the laws of the requested State. This might occur, for example, when individuals engaged in professional practices, such as law, are not required to keep books and records for Swiss purposes but are required to do so for U.S. tax purposes. The Protocol requires the requested State to treat the record-keeping requirements of the other State as its own in determining whether tax fraud exists. This provision applies to a profession or business, including to one conducted through a sole proprietorship, partnership or similar enterprise.

Paragraph 1 states that, in regard to tax fraud, information exchange is not restricted by Article 1 (Personal Scope). Accordingly, the requested State is obligated to provide information under this Article with respect to persons who are not residents of either State in cases where one of the Contracting States has alleged facts that would constitute tax fraud. For example, if a third-country resident has a permanent establishment in Switzerland and that permanent establishment engages in transactions with a U.S. enterprise, Switzerland would be obligated to provide information with respect to that permanent establishment, so long as the request indicated that the transactions involved tax fraud, even though the enterprise of which the permanent establishment is a part is not a resident of either State. Similarly, if a third-country resident maintains a bank account in Switzerland, and the Internal Revenue Service has reason to believe that the records of that account are relevant to a matter involving tax fraud, Switzerland would be obligated to provide the records of the account upon request by U.S. authorities.

Paragraph 1 provides that authenticated copies of unedited original records or documents shall be provided under this Article if specifically requested by the competent authority of the other Contracting State. Paragraph 8(b) of the Memorandum of Understanding clarifies that the term "records or documents" as used in this Article is an all-inclusive term. It covers all forms of recorded information whether held by public or private individuals or entities.

The provision of authenticated copies of unedited original records or documents in admissible form represents a substantial increase in the type of information available under the Convention. Because paragraph 1 of Article XVI of the prior Convention did not specifically refer to the form in which information could be exchanged, a Swiss Supreme Court decision limited the form of the information that the Swiss competent authorities could supply to the United States to reports and summaries of information.

Information (including bank records) that is obtained under the tax treaty may be used in any U.S. tax proceeding, whether civil or criminal. When such information is obtained under the Swiss law on International Mutual Assistance in Criminal Matters (known as "IMAC"), it may be used only in criminal tax cases because of the Swiss law of "speciality". This rule prevents tax authorities from using evidence previously obtained for one purpose from being used for another purpose. Thus, tax authorities currently may not use evidence of a tax crime that was received under IMAC for purposes of a civil matter, unless there has already been a conviction for the tax fraud that was the basis of the assistance. Under the Convention, even though the U.S. tax authorities will only receive information (other than information relating to the implementation of the Convention) if they are investigating or prosecuting a charge of tax fraud, the information may be used for a civil case, if the charge constituting tax fraud does not result in a conviction or the criminal investigation or prosecution is dropped.

Under current Swiss law, the Swiss tax authorities may not take depositions of persons in regard to any tax matters including Swiss domestic taxes. Such type of information would be available through other legal means applicable to assistance between the Contracting States, such as IMAC or the U.S.-Switzerland Mutual Legal Assistance Treaty ("MLAT") with respect to organized crime. Because certain types of information may still be obtained only under IMAC or the MLAT, Paragraph 8(a) of the Memorandum of Understanding reflects the understanding of the negotiators that the definition of tax fraud provided in the Protocol also applies when such other means of mutual legal assistance are used in matters involving tax fraud.

Paragraph 1 also provides assurances that any information exchanged will be treated as secret, subject to the same disclosure constraints as information obtained under the laws of the requesting State. Paragraph 1 provides additional disclosure constraints by requiring that information received may be disclosed only to persons, including courts and administrative bodies, concerned with the assessment, collection, enforcement or prosecution in respect of the taxes to which the information relates, or to persons concerned with the administration of those taxes. The information must be used by these persons in connection with these designated functions. Persons in the United States concerned with the administration of taxes include legislative bodies, such as the tax-writing committees of Congress and the General Accounting Office. Information received by these bodies must be for use in the performance of their role in overseeing the administration of U.S. tax laws. Paragraph 8(c) of the Memorandum of Understanding clarifies that the persons authorized to receive information may disclose the information in public court proceedings or in judicial decisions.

Paragraph 2

Paragraph 2 provides for assistance in collection of taxes to the extent necessary to ensure that treaty benefits under Articles 10 (Dividends), 11 (Interest), 12 (Royalties) and 18 (Pensions and Annuities) are enjoyed only by persons entitled to those benefits under the terms of the Convention. Under paragraph 2, a Contracting State may collect on behalf of the other State only those amounts necessary to ensure that any exemption or reduced rate of tax at source granted under the specified Articles of the Convention by that other State is not enjoyed by persons not entitled to those benefits. For example, Switzerland may withhold an additional 15 percent on a U.S. source dividend paid through a Swiss nominee where the beneficial owner of the stock was not entitled to benefits under the Convention. Switzerland has in fact undertaken such withholding pursuant to identical wording found in paragraph 2 of Article XVI of the prior Convention.

Paragraph 3

Paragraph 3 (along with the last sentence of paragraph 1) is in substance identical to paragraph 2 of Article 26 of the OECD Model. It provides that the obligations undertaken in paragraph 1 to exchange information do not require a Contracting State obligation to carry out administrative measures that are at variance with the regulations and practice of either Contracting State or contrary to its sovereignty, security or public policy. Nor is a Contracting State required to supply particulars not procurable under the laws of either Contracting State. Under the last sentence of paragraph 1, a Contracting State is not required to disclose any trade, business, industrial or professional secret or any trade process.

However, paragraph 8(d) of the Memorandum of Understanding makes clear that Swiss bank secrecy laws (and, therefore, paragraph 3) do not hinder the gathering of documentary evidence from banks, or its forwarding to the U.S. competent authority, in cases of tax fraud under this Article.

Paragraph 4

Paragraph 4 relates to the arbitration provisions of paragraph 6 of Article 25 (Mutual Agreement Procedure). When a case is referred to an arbitration board, confidential information necessary for carrying out the arbitration procedure may be released by the States to the board. The members of the board, and any staff, however, are subject to the disclosure rules of this Article.

Treaty effective dates and termination in relation to competent authority dispute resolution

A tax administration may seek information with respect to a year for which a treaty was in force after the treaty has been terminated. In such a case the ability of the competent authorities to act is limited. They may not exchange confidential information without the authority provided by the tax treaty.

The competent authority also may seek information under the Convention, but with respect to a year with respect to which the prior Convention was in force. If the Convention provides for greater exchange of information in a case than the prior Convention would provide, the scope of the competent authority's ability to exchange information is not constrained by the fact that the Convention was not in force when the transactions at issue occurred, and the competent authorities have available to them the full range of information exchange provisions afforded under this Article.

Article 27 (Members of Diplomatic Missions and Consular Posts)

The purpose of Article 27 is to ensure that diplomatic agents or consular officers shall, under the provisions of the Convention, receive no less favorable treatment than that to which they are entitled under international law or under special international agreements.

Paragraph 1

Paragraph 1 provides that any fiscal privileges to which diplomatic or consular officials are entitled under general provisions of international law or under special agreements will apply notwithstanding any provisions to the contrary in the Convention. The agreements referred to include any bilateral agreements, such as consular conventions, that affect the taxation of diplomats and consular officials and any multilateral agreements dealing with these issues, such as the Vienna Convention on Diplomatic Relations and the Vienna Convention on Consular Relations.

This paragraph does not independently provide any benefits to diplomatic agents and consular officials. Article 19 (Government Service) does so, as do Code section 893 and a number of bilateral and multilateral agreements. Rather, the Article specifically reconfirms in this context the statement in paragraph 1 of Article 28 (Miscellaneous) that nothing in the tax treaty will operate to restrict any benefit accorded by the general rules of international law or with any of the other agreements referred to above. In the event that there is a conflict between the tax treaty and international law or such other treaties, under which the diplomatic agent or consular official is entitled to greater benefits under the latter, the latter laws or agreements shall have precedence. Conversely, if the tax treaty confers a greater benefit than another agreement, the affected person could claim the benefit of the tax treaty. Accordingly, if an international agreement provides that a host country may not tax the salary of a diplomatic official of the other Contracting State, the salary will be exempt from tax despite any provisions of the Convention that would allow the host country to tax the income.

Paragraph 2

Paragraph 2 prevents a diplomatic agent or consular official from avoiding taxation entirely on income that would otherwise be subject to tax by reserving to the sending country the right to tax income that is exempt as a result of privileges provided by international law. This rule might apply, for example, if a diplomatic agent who is accredited by Switzerland to the United States receives royalties or dividends from Swiss sources and is exempt under international law from taxation in the United States. If that person also is treated as a resident of the United States under Article 4 (Resident), without this rule he could receive an exemption from, or a reduction of, the Swiss tax imposed on the income as a result of applying the Convention, even though he is not subject to tax in the United States on the income. This rule does not affect the application of international law but, instead, modifies the terms of the Convention in order to prevent the elimination of tax in both Contracting States as a result of the application of international law.

Paragraph 3

Under paragraph 3, an individual who is a member of a diplomatic mission or consular post of one of the States, whether that mission or consular post is situated in the other Contracting State or in a third State, will be deemed to be a resident of the sending State if two conditions are met: (1) in accordance with international law the individual is not liable to tax in the receiving State on income from sources outside that State and (2) the individual is taxable by the sending State on his total income, on the same basis as are residents of that State. Thus, for example, a U.S. diplomat stationed in Germany, and owning portfolio stock in a Swiss company, would be eligible for a reduction in the Swiss withholding rate to 15% under Article 10 (Dividends) of the Convention, assuming the other requirements of the Article were met. Residence as determined under this paragraph will apply notwithstanding any result to the contrary from the application to such individual of the rules of Article 4 (Resident).

Paragraph 4

Paragraph 4 clarifies that the Convention does not apply to international organizations or to organs or officials of such organizations, or to members of diplomatic missions or consular posts of third States present in a State, if such persons are not taxable in either State on total income on the same basis as are residents of those States.

Relation to Other Articles

Pursuant to subparagraph 3(b) of Article 1 (Personal Scope), the saving clause of paragraph 4 of Article 1 does not apply to override any benefits of this Article available to an individual who is neither a citizen of the State granting the benefit nor, in the case of the United States, has immigrant status there.

Article 28 (Miscellaneous)

This Article contains a number of rules that apply throughout the Convention.

Paragraph 1

Paragraph 1, like the comparable provision of the U.S. Model, states the generally accepted relationship both between the Convention and domestic law and between the Convention and other agreements between the Contracting States (i.e., that no provision in the Convention may restrict any exclusion, exemption, deduction, credit or other benefit accorded by the tax laws of the Contracting States, or by any other agreement between the Contracting States). For example, if a deduction would be allowed under the Code in computing the taxable income of a resident of Switzerland, the deduction also is allowed to that person in computing taxable income under the Convention. Paragraph 1 also means that the Convention may not increase the tax burden on a resident of a Contracting State beyond the burden determined under domestic law. Thus, a right to tax given by the Convention cannot be exercised unless that right also exists under internal law. The relationship between the non-discrimination provisions of the Convention and other agreements is not addressed in paragraph 1 but in paragraph 2.

It follows that, under the principle of paragraph 1, a taxpayer's liability to U.S. tax need not be determined under the Convention if the Code would produce a more favorable result. A taxpayer may not, however, choose among the provisions of the Code and the Convention in an inconsistent manner in order to minimize tax. For example, assume that a resident of Switzerland has three separate businesses in the United States. One is a profitable permanent establishment and the other two are trades or businesses that would earn income that would be taxable under the Code but that do not meet the permanent establishment threshold tests of the Convention. One is profitable and the other incurs a loss. Under the Convention, the income of the permanent establishment is taxable, and both the profit and the loss of the other two businesses are ignored. Under the Code, all three would be subject to tax, but the loss would be offset against the profits of the two profitable ventures. The taxpayer may not invoke the Convention to exclude the profits of the profitable trade or business and invoke the Code to offset the loss of the loss trade or business against the profit of the permanent establishment. (See Rev. Rul. 84-17, 1984-1 C.B. 10.) If, however, the taxpayer invokes the Code for the taxation of all three ventures, the taxpayer would not be precluded from invoking the Convention with respect to, for example, any dividend income the taxpayer may receive from the United States that is not effectively connected with any of his business activities in the United States.

Similarly, nothing in the Convention can be used to deny any benefit granted by any other agreement between the United States and Switzerland. If, for example, there were a Status of Forces Agreement between the United States and Switzerland, benefits provided for military personnel or military contractors under such agreement would be available to residents of the Contracting States regardless of any provisions to the contrary (or silence) in the Convention.

Paragraph 2

Paragraph 2 specifically relates to non-discrimination obligations of the Contracting States under other agreements. The provisions of paragraph 2 are an exception to the rule provided in paragraph 1 of this Article under which the Convention shall not restrict in any manner any exclusion, exemption, deduction, credit or other allowance now or hereafter accorded by any other agreement between the Contracting States.

Subparagraph (a) of paragraph 2 provides that, notwithstanding any other agreement to which the Contracting States may be parties, a dispute concerning whether a measure is within the scope of the Convention shall be considered only by the competent authorities of the Contracting States, and the procedures under the Convention exclusively shall apply to the dispute. Thus, procedures for dealing with disputes that may be incorporated into trade, investment, or other agreements between the Contracting States shall not apply for the purpose of determining the scope of the Convention.

Subparagraph (b) of paragraph 2 provides that, unless the competent authorities determine that a taxation measure is not within the scope of the Convention, the nondiscrimination obliga-tions of this Convention exclusively shall apply with respect to that measure, except for such national treatment or most-favored-nation ("MFN") obligations as may apply to trade in goods under the General Agreement on Tariffs and Trade ("GATT"). No national treatment or MFN obligation under any other agreement shall apply with respect to that measure. Thus, unless the competent authorities agree otherwise, any national treatment and MFN obligations undertaken by the Contracting States under agreements other than the Convention shall not apply to a taxation measure, with the exception of GATT as applicable to trade in goods.

Subparagraph (c) of paragraph 2 defines a "measure" broadly. It would include, for example, a law, regulation, rule, procedure, decision, administrative action, or any other form of governmental guidance.

Paragraph 3

Paragraph 3 incorporates into the Convention the rule of Code section 864(c)(6). Like the Code section on which it is based, paragraph 3 provides that any income or gain attributable to a permanent establishment or a fixed base during its existence is taxable in the Contracting State where the permanent establishment or fixed base is situated even if that income or gain is deferred until after the permanent establishment or fixed base ceases to exist. Paragraph 3 also clarifies that expenses attributable to the permanent establishment or fixed base during its existence may be deducted from the deferred income at such time as that income is subject to tax. This rule applies with respect to paragraphs 1 and 2 of Article 7 (Business Profits), paragraph 5 of Article 10 (Dividends), paragraph 3 of Article 12 (Royalties), paragraph 3 of Article 13 (Gains), paragraph 2 of Article 14 (Independent Personal Services), and paragraph 2 of Article 21 (Other Income). The preceding rule regarding the taxation of deferred income and the allowance of appropriate expenses against such income will not affect any rules in the internal laws of the States relating to the accrual of income and expenses. For example, income arising from an installment sale that is recognized for U.S. tax purposes in years subsequent to the year of the sale will be recognized in accordance with section 453 of the Code.

The effect of this rule can be illustrated by the following example. Assume a company that is a resident of Switzerland and that maintains a permanent establishment in the United States winds up the permanent establishment's business and sells the permanent establishment's inventory and assets to a U.S. buyer at the end of year 1 in exchange for an interest-bearing installment obligation payable in full at the end of year 3. Despite the fact that Article 13's threshold requirement for U.S. taxation is not met in year 3 because the company has no permanent establishment in the United States, the United States may tax the deferred income payment recognized by the company in year 3.

Paragraph 4

Paragraph 4 deals with cross-border pension contributions in order to prevent any failure of the two Contracting States' laws regarding the deductibility of pension contributions to mesh properly from inhibiting the flow of personal services between the Contracting States. Many countries allow deductions or exclusions to their residents for contributions, made by them or on their behalf, to resident pension plans, but do not allow deductions or exclusions for payments made to plans resident in another country, even if the structure and legal requirements of such plans in the two countries are similar.

Paragraph 4 allows for the deductibility or exclusion in one State of contributions to a "recognized" plan or arrangement in the other if certain conditions are satisfied. A recognized plan is one that is recognized for purposes of determining the tax liability of the person making the contribution or on whose behalf the contribution is made (i.e., a plan the contributions to which may be taken as a deduction or excluded from income) or one whose income is exempt from taxation. Recognized retirement plans include, for example, a Keough Plan and an Individual Retirement Account.

The benefit of this paragraph is allowed to an individual who is present in one of the Contracting States to perform either dependent or independent personal services. The individual, however, must be a visitor to the host country. Therefore, he can receive the benefit only if he has been present there for no more than five years at the time he is claiming the benefit. The host-country competent authority must determine that the recognized plan to which a contribution is made in the home country of the individual generally corresponds to the plan in the host country. The individual must have been contributing to the plan in his home country, or to a plan that was replaced by the plan to which he is contributing, before coming to the host country. The allowance of a successor plan would apply if, for example, the employer has been taken over by another corporation that replaces the existing plan with its own plan, rolling membership in the old plan over into the new plan. Finally, the benefits under this paragraph are limited to the benefits that the host country accords to plans recognized under its law, even if the home country would have afforded greater benefits under its law. Thus, for example, if the host country has a cap on contributions equal to five percent of the remuneration, and the home country has a seven percent cap, the deduction is limited to five percent, even though the individual would have been allowed to take the larger deduction if he had remained in his home country.

This provision follows closely model text provided in the Commentary to the 1992 OECD Model. It does not, however, include other benefits that are provided by the comparable provision in the U.S. Model (a deduction for contributions to the plan for purposes of computing the employer's taxable income in the State where the individual renders services, an exemption from tax on undistributed earnings realized by the plan, and exemption from tax on rollovers from one plan to another).

Paragraph 5

Paragraph 5 is intended to deal with changes in law of either of the Contracting States that have the effect of changing the application of the Convention in a significant manner or that alter the relationship between the Contracting States. Paragraph 5 provides, first, that, in response to a change in the law of either State, the appropriate authority of either State may request consultations with its counterpart in the other State to determine whether a change in the Convention is appropriate. The "appropriate authorities" may be the Contracting States them-selves, communicating through diplomatic channels, or they may be the competent authorities under the Convention, communicating directly. The request for consultations may come either from the authority of the Contracting State making the change in law, or it may come from the authority of the other State. If the authorities determine, on the basis of the consultations, that a change in domestic legislation has significantly altered the balance of benefits provided by the Convention, they will consult with a view to amending the Convention to restore an appropriate balance. Any such amendment would, of course, require a protocol or new treaty which would be subject to Senate advice and consent to ratification.

Article 29 (Entry into Force)

This Article contains the rules for bringing the Convention into force and giving effect to its provisions.

Paragraph 1

Paragraph 1 provides for the ratification of the Convention by both Contracting States according to their constitutional and statutory procedures.

In the United States, the process leading to ratification and entry into force of the Convention is as follows: Once the Convention has been signed by authorized representatives of the two Contracting States, the Department of State sends the Convention to the President who formally transmits it to the Senate for its advice and consent to ratification, which requires approval by two-thirds of the Senators present and voting. After receiving the advice and consent of the Senate to ratification, the Convention is returned to the President. The President is thus authorized to complete the process by signing the U.S. instrument of ratification, and then exchanging the instruments with the other Contracting State.

Paragraph 2

Paragraph 2 provides that the Convention will enter into force upon the exchange of instruments of ratification. The date on which a treaty enters into force is not necessarily the date on which its provisions take effect. Paragraph 2, therefore, also contains rules that determine when the provisions of the treaty will have effect. Under paragraph 2(a), the Convention will have effect with respect to taxes withheld at source (principally investment income, such as dividends, interest and royalties, and social security benefits) for amounts paid or credited on or after the first day of the second month following the date on which the Convention enters into force. For example, if instruments of ratification are exchanged on April 25 of a given year, the elimination of withholding tax at source on interest provided by paragraph 1 of Article 11 (Interest) would be applicable to any interest paid or credited on or after June 1 of that year. This rule allows the benefits of the withholding reductions to be put into effect as soon as possible, without waiting until the following year. The delay of one to two months is required to allow sufficient time for withholding agents to be informed about the change in withholding rates. If for some reason a withholding agent withholds at a higher rate than that provided by the Convention (perhaps because it was not able to re-program its computers before the payment is made), the beneficial owner of the income may make a claim for refund pursuant to section 1464.

For all other taxes, paragraph 2(b) specifies that the Convention will have effect for any taxable year or assessment period beginning on or after January 1 of the year following entry into force. Because the federal excise tax on insurance premiums is collected quarterly and is not a withholding tax, the effective date provided by paragraph 2(b) will apply to that tax.

Paragraph 3

As in many recent U.S. treaties, the Paragraph 3 provides a "grace period" in the form of a general exception to the effective date rules of paragraph 2. Under this paragraph, if the prior Convention would have afforded greater relief from tax to a person entitled to its benefits than would be the case under this Convention, that person may elect to remain subject to all of the provisions of the prior Convention for a twelve-month period from the date on which this Convention would have had effect under the provisions of paragraph 2 of this Article. During the period in which the election is in effect, the provisions of the prior Convention will continue to apply only insofar as they applied prior to the entry into force of the Convention.

For example, under the Convention a non-publicly-traded corporation resident in the other Contracting State that is wholly-owned by third-country residents and that earns portfolio dividends from passive investments in the United States would be denied U.S. treaty benefits with respect to those dividends under the provisions of Article 22 (Limitation on Benefits). Assuming that the prior Convention contained no anti-treaty-shopping rule, so that the corporation would be entitled to the reduced U.S. withholding rate of 15 percent, this corporation may elect under the grace period rule to be subject to the rules of the prior Convention for one additional year from the effective date specified in paragraph 2(a), thereby receiving U.S. treaty benefits for that period. This rule gives those residents of a Contracting State that would be entitled to benefits under the prior Convention but would not be as a result of the application of the Limitation on Benefits provision of the Convention an additional year to restructure their activities in a manner that would entitle them to qualify for benefits. Under the prior Convention, foreign source income attributable to a U.S. permanent establishment was not subject to U.S. tax. If a Swiss resident has a U.S. permanent establishment that earns Canadian source income, that income would be exempt under the prior Convention, but taxable under the Convention. The Swiss resident claiming that the Canadian-source income is exempt may do so for one additional year after the first taxable year beginning on or after the first day of January following entry into force of the new treaty.

If the grace period is elected, all of the provisions of the prior Convention must be applied for that additional year. The taxpayer may not apply certain, more favorable, provisions of the prior Convention and, at the same time, apply other, more favorable, provisions of the Convention. Thus, a Swiss enterprise with a permanent establishment in the United States cannot rely on the prior Convention to avoid the branch profits tax and at the same time claim exemption from the branch level interest tax on excess interest on the basis that Article 11 (Interest) of the Convention eliminates source-basis taxation of interest (and therefore the excess interest tax). The enterprise must choose one regime or the other.

Paragraph 4

Paragraph 4 provides a rule to coordinate the termination of the prior Convention with the effective dates of the new treaty. The prior Convention will cease to have effect when the provisions of this Convention take effect in accordance with paragraphs 2 and 3 of the Article. Thus, for a person not taking advantage of the election in paragraph 3, the prior Convention will cease to have effect at the time, on or after January 1 of the year following entry into force of the Convention, when the provisions of the new Convention first have effect. For persons electing the additional year of coverage of the prior Convention, the prior Convention will remain in effect for one additional year beyond the date specified in the preceding sentence.

Relation to Other Articles

Paragraph 4 is excepted from the saving clause of paragraph 2 of Article 1 (Personal Scope) with respect to persons who are neither citizens nor have immigrant status in the United States. Thus, the United States will allow Swiss residents who are also U.S. residents under the Code to deduct contributions made to Swiss pension funds if the requirements of paragraph 4 are satisfied.

Article 30 (Termination)

This provision generally corresponds to its counterpart in the OECD Model. The Convention is to remain in effect indefinitely, unless terminated by one of the States in accordance with the provisions of Article 30. The Convention may be terminated by either State at any time, provided that at least six months' prior written notice has been given through diplomatic channels. If notice is given on or before June 30 of any calendar year, the termination will have effect as follows: (1) with respect to taxes withheld at source on dividends, interest, and royalties, the Convention will cease to have effect for amounts paid or credited on or after January 1 of the calendar year following the year in which the notice is given (subparagraph (a)); and (2) with respect to other taxes, the Convention will cease to have effect for taxable years or assessment periods beginning on or after January 1 of the calendar year following the year in which notice is given (subparagraph (b)).

A treaty performs certain specific and necessary functions regarding information exchange and mutual agreement. In the case of information exchange the treaty's function is to override confidentiality rules relating to taxpayer information. In the case of mutual agreement, its function is to allow competent authorities to modify internal law in order to avoid double taxation. With respect to the effective termination dates for these aspects of the treaty, therefore, if a treaty is terminated as of January 1 of a given year, no otherwise confidential information can be exchanged after that date, regardless of whether the treaty was in force for the taxable year to which the request relates. Similarly, no mutual agreement departing from internal law can be implemented after that date, regardless of the taxable year to which the agreement relates. Therefore, for the competent authorities to be allowed to exchange otherwise confidential information or to reach a mutual agreement that departs from internal law, a treaty must be in force at the time those actions are taken.

Article 30 relates only to unilateral termination of the Convention by a Contracting State. Nothing in that Article should be construed as preventing the Contracting States from concluding a new bilateral agreement, subject to ratification, that supersedes, amends or terminates provisions of the Convention without the six month notification period.

Customary international law, as reflected in the Vienna Convention on Treaties, allows termination by one Contracting State at any time in the event of a "material breach" of the agreement by the other Contracting State.